SEASONED FOR THIS SEASON!

REFLECTIONS FOR *SEASONED* SINGLES

JERI DARBY

ARARITY PRESS

Copyright @ 2018 by Jeri Darby

All rights reserved. In accordance with the U.S. Copyright Act of 1976, the scanning, uploading, and electronic sharing of any part of this book without the permission of the publisher is unlawful piracy and theft of the author's intellectual property. If you would like to use material from this book (other than for review purposes), prior written permission must be obtained by contacting the publisher at araritypress@gmail.com

Unless otherwise indicated all scripture quotations are taken from KJV.

Scriptures taken from the Holy Bible, New International Version®, NIV®. Copyright © 1973, 1978, 1984, 2011 by Biblica, Inc.™ Used by permission of Zondervan. All rights reserved worldwide.

Scriptures marked NLT are taken from the HOLY BIBLE, NEW LIVING TRANSLATION (NLT): Scriptures taken from the HOLY BIBLE, NEW LIVING TRANSLATION, Copyright ©1996, 2004, 2007 by Tyndale House Foundation. Used by permission of Tyndale House Publishers, Inc., Carol Stream, Illinois 60188. All rights reserved. Used by permission.

"Scripture quotations taken from the New American Standard Bible®, Copyright © 1960, 1962, 1963, 1968, 1971, 1972, 1973, 1975, 1977, 1995 by The Lockman Foundation Used by permission." (www.Lockman.org)

Seasoned for This Season!
Reflections for *Seasoned* Singles

by
Jeri Darby

ISBN-0997939915 (Ararity Press)
ISBN-9780997939910

Ararity Press
araritypress@gmail.com
989 717-1031
Facebook: Jeri Darby

Dedication

This book is dedicated to:
Jesus Christ, who is the Author and Finisher of my faith.
The One who kept His commitment to *never* leave or forsake me.

The Holy Spirit, my Comforter, Counselor, Personal Assistant and my *Very Best* Friend.

To the Eternal, Immortal, Invisible and the Only Wise God, my Heavenly Father, Creator who is my Endless Source and Sustainer.

Preface

I am called and chosen by the Most High God. I am honored to be the King's daughter! *Nevertheless,* I struggle. Sara Davidson wrote, "And yet, all these years I'd been terrified I would be stoned to death if people saw through the façade." I am sixty-four years old and know firsthand what she is saying. Most of my life has been spent trying to camouflage perceived flaws. During earlier years I longed to fit into popular clicks and I battled feelings of unworthiness.

Stupid blunders, idiotic mistakes, regrets and humiliating situations of my youth often parade through my head— all at once! When struck by the reality of their costly penalties—I sway from the invisible weight. When expressing that our true selves will *never* be *good enough*—satan can be quite convincing. The love of my Father, God has taught me to embrace and cherish my uniqueness. It took years to grasp this wisdom and I cling to it while venturing into seasoned years.

Whether male or female; the fear of *never* making a special connection may cause your insides to quiver. Satan will plant thoughts that you are unworthy, or God has forgotten about you. Don't be deceived. We are sons and daughters of the King of King's—God will *never* toss us into a discount section because of age or any other reason. The price of His daughters is yet *far-rrrrr* above rubies and His sons are His mighty men of valor! Desiring companionship is God's natural order, *at any age*—don't apologize! Don't stop believing God for someone special. Marriage is honorable in all seasons of life.

This book is *not* meant to be a how-to date, how to get a mate, treat a mate, keep a mate or a guide for social etiquettes. Its brief writings are intended to spark introspection and exploration of your inner world. Take this opportunity to examine your thoughts and underlying emotions. This process will enable you to move forward with greater clarity. Life is a journey of continuous growth and spiritual development while learning to lean and depend on God.

Over the years, God has been my Help, my Strength and Sustainer. The support of my Father God is unrelenting. His love steadfast and His mercies fresh and new each morning. He will *always* love and treasure us in every season of our life—*whether young or seasoned, whether married or single...*

Time moves forward, whether we choose to or not. As we grow older the ability to rebound, adjust and keep moving becomes even more critical.

Acknowledgements

Years ago, God planted in my spirit the desire to publish books—many books! My response was, "God I don't know the first step."

He replied, "I will have someone there to guide you each step of the way." I often allowed distractions to kidnap my attention and snatch me off the path for years at a time. God has been Faithful. Whenever I re-emerged demonstrating the willingness and readiness to move forward He *always* had someone to impart new knowledge and encouragement.

Today I extend thanks to all my family, children, grandchildren and friends who showered me with generous words of encouragement. Special thanks to Patricia Hampton whom I'm provoking to free her inner author. To Sheryln Miller who mentored me through the self-publication process of my first book and continues to offer selfless support.

To my daughter Yolonda Brown-Stanley who brain stormed, edited, provided loads of emotional support and anything else needed. Yolonda is an amazing author whose books will someday bring emotional healing to many!

After the publication of my first book, "Stepping Stones, Reflections for Single's," I stood in the reality of the truth that... writing a book is the *easy* part. After that the *real* work begins. I am grateful for connecting with my gifted writing coach, Sandra N. Peoples. She has provided a wealth of information to equip me with continuing the author's journey.

I thank readers of "Stepping Stones, Reflections for Single's, Volume I" who provided feedback about how my book impacted their lives. The writing ministry is all about touching lives. I am grateful that God entrusted me with this assignment and it is my intent to glorify Him and all I say, do and write.

*I
Am using the
Stepping Stones
In my life
To soar into my destiny...
While helping
Others along the way!*

Table of Contents

Selfie (ME)	Page 1
Selfies	Page 2
Annals	Page 4
Prophetic Decrees	Pages 5, 6
Testimony	Page 7
Stretch	Page 9
Ticking	Page 11
Bushido	Page 13
Quickie	Page 15
Giddy	Page 17
Moses	Page 19
Song	Page 21
Boobs	Page 23
Integrity	Page 25
Selfie(Confession)	Page 27
Liars	Page 29
Signals	Page 31
Who	Page 33
Standards	Page 35
Query	Page 37
Circulation	Page 39
Accepted	Page 41
Might	Page 43
Impeccable	Page 45
Spice	Page 47
Selfie (He Knew)	Page 49
Issues	Page 51
Online.com	Page 53
HTN	Page 55
Gossip	Page 57
Impasse	Page 59
Jealousy	Page 61
Knowledge	Page 63
Murmuring	Page 65

Table of Contents (Continued)

Chosen	Page 67
Despair	Page 69
Selfie (Brighter Days)	Page 71
Connecting	Page 73
Laughter	Page 75
Drudgery	Page 77
Retired	Page 79
Fruitful	Page 81
Balance	Page 83
Struggling	Page 85
Respect	Page 87
Marriage	Page 89
Why?	Page 93
Me!	Page 94
Swords	Page 95
Vows	Page 97
Selfie (Nevertheless)	Page 99
Beauty	Page 101
Victorious	Page 103
Counselor	Page 105
Rest	Page 107
Encouragement	Page 109
Peace	Page 111
Fireproof	Page 113
Menopause	Page 115
Cake	Page 117
Prayer	Page 119
Addictions	Page 121
Selfie (Clarity)	Page 123
Treasures	Page 125
Incredible	Page 127
Straight	Page 129

Table of Contents (Continued)

Rebound	Page 131
Disabilities	Page 133
Kisses	Page 135
Legitimate	Page 137
Praise	Page 139
Interruptions	Page 141
Selfie (Holy Excitement)	Page 143
Feelings	Page 145
Elephants	Page 147
College	Page 149
Therefore	Page 151
Pain	Page 153
Epiphany	Page 155
Birth	Page 157
Offence	Page 159
Accommodation	Page 161
Selfie (War)	Page 163
Quotation	Page 165
About the Author	Page 166
A Prayer for You	Page 167
Write Your Personal Prayer	Page 168
Other Books by Jeri Darby	Pages 169, 170
Thank You	Page 171

Simply

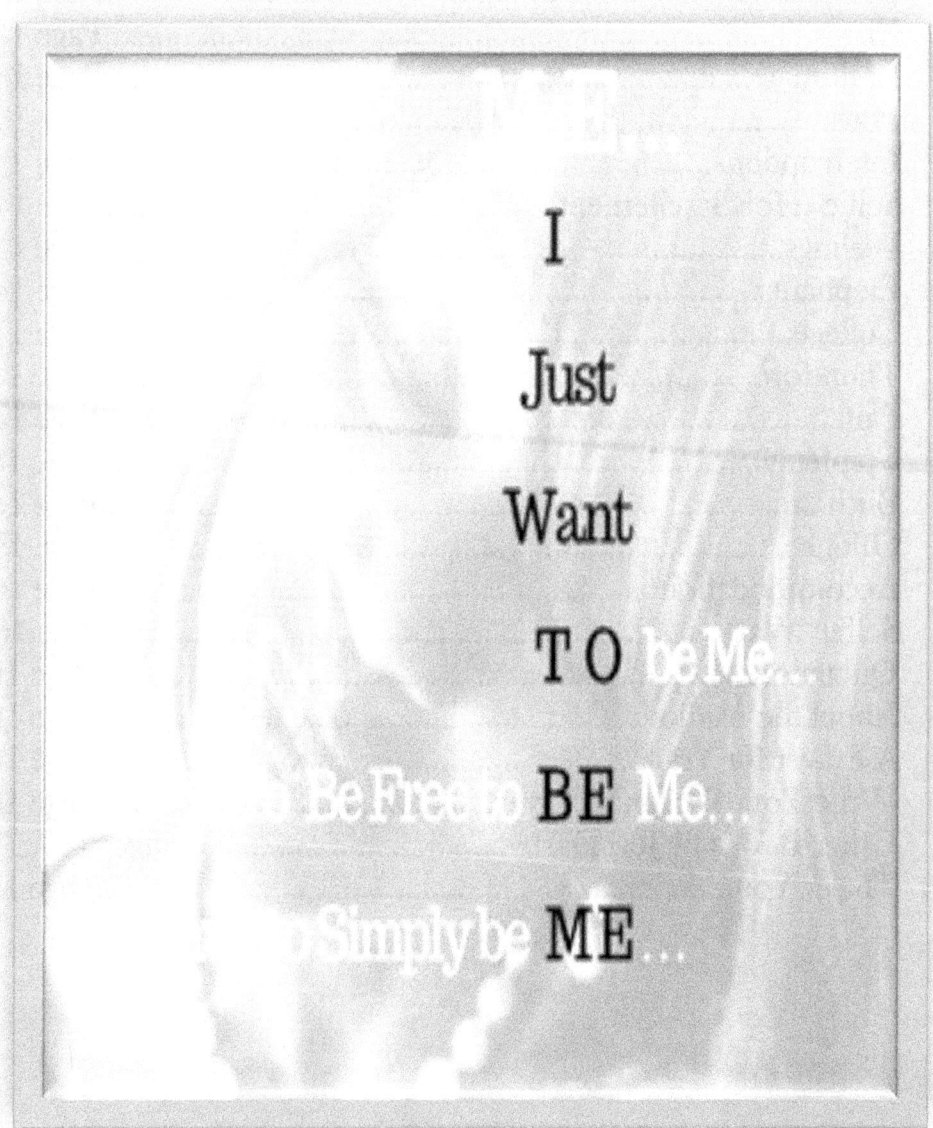

I

Just

Want

TO be Me...

Be Free to BE Me...

Simply be ME...

Selfies

"Let's take a selfie!" I suggested to a friend who I met for lunch."

"Sure." *Lights! Camera! Action!* Before leaving the restaurant, we posed, snapped, giggled and deleted and deleted and deleted...and deleted photo after photo. Forty shots later we still felt uncomfortable with our photo options to post on Facebook. We accepted defeat. I have shared similar experiences when out with other friends. Either they refuse photos or frown at the selections while stating that none are suitable.

There's a condition called body dysmorphic disorder. This describes a person who is preoccupied with their perceived imperfections. This can cause aversion to photo images or constant self-demeaning remarks directed toward themselves when looking at their picture. Could this be the root of mine and my other friends problem?

Perhaps ours and many others who run from cameras. *Always* armed with excuses, I managed to successfully escape being photographed for years. "I don't take good photos! The camera doesn't like me. No! don't post *that* picture!" Then I view lovely photos of others posing with family, friends or sharing personal milestones with much regret. At age 64, I wish I had been more cooperate with allowing photographs. I have finally began easing up. The absence of a photogenic history recording the journey of my younger years brings feelings of remorse.

Photos are a precious gift to leave for our children and grandchildren and coming generations that will *never* get to meet us—in the flesh. This book includes selfies all taken at the age of 64 with inspirational thoughts. They mark the end of my "scopophobia" (which is fear of being photographed). Pictures were included to illustrate my newly discovered freedom and commitment in this area.

I wish to impart this newfound freedom to my readers. It is common to zero in on our imperfections and even magnify them until any positive qualities are overshadowed or completely obliterated in our minds. It is difficult to walk in true authenticity while despising your image captured in a photograph or peering back through the mirror. If this has been your struggle, I pray that you to will find enough peace to *stop* avoiding *every* photo opportunity. The ability to embrace and accept your photo image is a stepping stone towards self-acceptance.

Annals

Did you know that King Josiah was eight years old when he became king? He was the youngest king in the bible. I love reading about the kings of biblical times. After sharing some details and history of their reign, the reader is referred to the book of Annals for more details. What are annals? They are books where the historical events of the king's reign are logged. Basically, we are talking about some sort of journal. The Bible refers to God's people *(US)* as kings and priests. Just like the biblical kings, we need annals! Why record annals? Annals document the significant events of our life.

My annals are sporadic, sketchy and scrawled inside years of scattered notebooks. I wish I had been more organized and consistent as I am amnesic when it comes to recalling dates and past events with clarity. Severe trauma and dysfunction during early years deprived me of most of my childhood memories. To be truthful, I am not great with recalling adulthood memories either. I enjoy reading journals from my past. I very much regret not exercising more discipline in this area. Listed below are a few benefits I have discovered through journaling.

> **Emotional clarity**
> **Inspired Songs, Articles, Books & Sermons**
> **Holy Spirit inspired answers to questions**
> **A reservoir for easily retrievable memories**
> **Healing for childhood traumas**
> **Creative business ideas**
> **And much, much more...**

Over the years I have advised many to engage in the journaling process some have continued and later thanked me. The wisdom that emerges from the simple act of journaling will amaze you. There are blank pages following each of the writings in this book. For those who get writer's block from staring at blank pages—I have included writing prompts to jumpstart your thoughts. Start your Annals- *TODAY!*

My Prophetic Decrees

Thou shalt also decree a thing and it shall be established.
Job 22:28 KJV

Initially, this page was titled *"Affirmations."* Affirmations are statements affirming that something is true. Then I heard the word *"Decrees."* Both are effective practices; but decrees extend beyond mere agreement. We are God's kings and priests. (Revelation 1:6) Decrees are spoken from a position of power and authority linked to our divine identity. We decree things that have not yet manifested in the physical with great anticipation because of *who* we are and *whose* we are.

Pray about what you desire God to make a reality in your life as it relates to singleness or *any* matter. Take time to create your list, there is no need to complete it in one day. Jot them down as they rise in your spirit.

Write your prophetic decrees on these pages and speak them aloud daily. *"Date"* is purposely included on both ends in order to record the day you *begin* decreeing and the date it was *established.* Let's exercise and challenge our faith by fully utilizing the power of our words!

Date Decreed   Date Established

_____ *I Decree* _____

_____ *I Decree* _____

_____ *I Decree* _____

_____ *I Decree* _____

_____ *I Decree* _____

_____ *I Decree* _____

Date Decreed		Date Established
_____	*I Decree* _____	
_____	*I Decree* _____	
_____	*I Decree* _____	
_____	*I Decree* _____	
_____	*I Decree* _____	
_____	*I Decree* _____	
_____	*I Decree* _____	
_____	*I Decree* _____	
_____	*I Decree* _____	
_____	*I Decree* _____	
_____	*I Decree* _____	
_____	*I Decree* _____	
_____	*I Decree* _____	
_____	*I Decree* _____	
_____	*I Decree* _____	

Testimony

"One of the most important ways we nourish our testimonies is by sharing them with others. Sharing our testimonies not only builds others but brings greater "light" and further blessings into our own lives."
Spencer W. Kimball

Testimonies, we all have them. God will use them to encourage others—if we dare to share when He prompts. The longer we live; the more likely we have experienced atrocious satanic attacks. Our survival is confirmation of God's grace in our lives. Testimonies encourages others to keep breathing, hang on and move forward another day. You are evidence that there is hope despite foolish mistakes and painful experiences. "God, you *sure*?" I've questioned when I'm nudged to share while writing for publication, public speaking or livestreaming. Transparency is an ongoing struggle that gets easier over time.

Openness is a challenge; we live in such a judgmental era. I describe myself as *private* and many would consider me overly hush-hush. Let's face it- this is the age of the web, cloud and cell phone cameras with live streaming everywhere- privacy is a joke! Illusions of privacy are demolished. Life is a warzone! Once we have won a few battles- we are equipped to lead others to victories! Testimonies are strategic spiritual weapons—once this is understood— then sharing becomes a joy.

Testimonies are those life experiences that validate the faithfulness of God in our lives to ourselves and others. They identify us as His witnesses upon the earth. They establish historical evidence of God's love, presence protection and provision. They are the fertilizer to a faith-filled spirit to keep it richly rooted in the promises of God. There is a single person out there that would benefit from you sharing your story. You hold the key to someone's deliverance. Grasp the courage to follow God's directive for when and how to release your testimony.

And they overcame him by the blood of the Lamb, and by the word of their testimony; and they loved not their lives unto the death.
Revelation 12:11 KJV

Thoughts

Are you withholding your testimony? If so, why?

S-T-R-E-T-C-H

What would you do today if you were not afraid?
Spencer Johnson

Too much of my life has rotted away in mundane, repetitive, autopilot, robotic, stagnant *existence.* Too many years have dwindled in successions of sunsets and sunrises—with little in between. Growing up; I internalized my mother's fears and mistakenly accepted them as mine.

Over the years her world shrunk, and she was contained within the walls of a tiny apartment peering out windows in her latter years. There were no lasting relationships; exploring new interests or venturing into the unknown. Her life fizzled in avoidance of anything outside her small circle of comfort.

I learned to press beyond inherent fears to some degree. I began setting regular stretch goals. A desire to actively participate in life plunged me beyond crippling non-involvement.

I never dreamed of public speaking, writing and entering the nursing profession. God continues stripping away my debilitating shyness as I continue to stretch. I have done TV and radio interviews and now host my own livestream vlog on social media sites to encourage others to *S-T-R-E-T-C-H.*

Singleness is not a sentence dooming one to isolation and non-involvement. Don't let more years vanish without trying something new! Life is a contact sport—the more players on the field, the more exciting the game. Do your warm up stretches; then jump in, participate, laugh, and have fun— as a *seasoned* single Christian!

> "Oh, that you would bless me and enlarge my territory! Let your hand be with me, and keep me from harm so that I will be free from pain."
> And God granted his request.
> I Chronicles 4:10 NIV

Thoughts

What areas do you feel the Holy Spirit stretching you? Are you resisting?

Ticking

You never want to have that ticking clock and know that you had all this time and didn't use it.
J.J. Abrams

A woman shared, "I'm the type of person willing to help anyone who desires a closer walk with God. I was excited about helping him. I bought him a bible like mine and we began reading scriptures on whatever issues he was struggling with.

This went on several weeks. At some point he began making comments about marriage. "I'm a Christian, you're a Christian—we should just go ahead and get married!" I joked about this initially but later I began giving it serious thought.

"I was 37 years old, and my biological clock was *ticking*. I started entertaining the possibility. He was not a bad looking guy, plus he was a great cook who could clean which was a bonus. I always said I wanted to be married by 40. Besides I hadn't had sex in years—I was ready!

Flimsy reasoning—*I know*. But he hammered away until I finally said 'yes." We managed to complete mandatory premarital classes offered by the health department though I cancelled three times. While praying about my decision *I knew* what God was saying. But I married him *anyways.*"

Such transparency! I admired her. Drugs and abuse soon entered the marriage. This woman was wise enough to exit—*quickly*— and filed for divorce after five months. Satan only approves marriage when it is to someone that will support his efforts to *destroy* you.

Biological clocks, loneliness, sexual frustrations and many other *flimsy* reasons can launch you onto a premature marital path. Marriage is among one of the most important decision you will make. Yes, you may be on the brink or even well into your seasoned years; but give marriage the prayer and consideration that it deserves! Then whatever God says—***do it!***

Look to the Lord and His strength, seek His face always.
I Chronicles 16:11 NIV

Thoughts

Are you on the brink of making a hasty decision because you feel like time is running out?

_____
_____
_____
_____
_____
_____
_____
_____
_____
_____
_____
_____
_____
_____
_____
_____
_____
_____
_____
_____

Bushido

*"Anyone can give up; it is the easiest thing in the world to do. But to hold it together when everyone would expect you to fall apart,
now that is true strength."*
Chris Bradford

"Mighty warrior with a spear," While reading the card with the meaning of my nickname, "Jeri," I smiled. This meaning describes my journey and reminds me of the term "Bushido," which is a Japanese word meaning *"the way of the warrior."*

Warrior. Isn't this an accurate depiction of the single life? Commitment to abstinence during the single journey— not an easy plight! For some singleness scans years— even decades! If you are not a warrior at the beginning—you will become one along the way. It's imperative to "fight the good fight of faith."

Abstinence is not a war against physical enemies; but battling against your own body's natural urges and inclinations. These are intensified by outside influences such as movies, media and music etc. It's a war against satanic whisperings aimed at disarming you such as, "your biological clock is ticking, you are getting *really* old or no one will *ever* want you!" It's a war against a culture that's sculptured for couples.

True, living single is not always easy and marriage can become over glamorized in our minds. Singles can fail to fully appreciate the tremendous spiritual warfare fought in marriages. Couples must also become warriors to create, maintain and protect their sacred unions.

I don't always feel like being a warrior- does anyone? Yet God is Faithful to provide grace and strength for this journey. He reloads fresh mercies each new day that we choose to go *the way of the warrior.* Seasoned single Christian warriors; you are not in this battle alone—though at times it may seem that way. God has a plan—*Trust Him.*

For the weapons of our warfare are not carnal, but mighty through God to the pulling down of strong holds;
2 Corinthians 10:4 KJV

Thoughts

What is the meaning of your name? How does it align with your purpose and destiny?

_____
_____
_____
_____
_____
_____
_____
_____
_____
_____
_____
_____
_____
_____
_____
_____
_____
_____
_____

Quickie

Something done or had quickly, especially sex or an alcoholic drink
Online Cambridge Dictionary

When I first received salvation, time eluded me when praying. Fond of basking in God's presence, I talked with Him for hours. When I read that Daniel prayed three times a day- so did I. It was a wonderful season of intimacy and learning God's voice with an ever-increasing awareness of His immense love— *for me.* This was pre-nursing career.

Over the years, time seemed to pass much quicker. On awakening I start my day racing with the clock. Once prepared for work I murmured a few words of prayer- *a quickie-* and I'm off! I know that there are other references to the word *"quickie."* The most common refers to the brevity of a sexual encounter. Nope, not that! I'm talking about prayer.

One of my deepest regrets over the years is that too often all I've managed to offer God in prayer is—yep, quickies. Our intimacy suffered greatly. The Holy Spirit has been coaching me in the art of slowing down while wooing me back into the presence of God. I find myself engaging in ongoing dialogue with Him about anything and everything as I go through hectic days.

Yet nothing on earth compares to finding a secluded spot to linger in the sweetness of the peace, love and joy found awaiting in His presence. God *never* tires of talking with us. *Never* becomes frustrated with spending time with us. *No one* in this world loves us so completely-or ever will! We are His beloved.

My beloved spake, and said unto me, Rise up, my love, my fair one,
and come away. Arise
Song of Solomon KJV

Thoughts

What is one thing you can start TODAY to increase intimate time spent with God?

_____
_____
_____
_____
_____
_____
_____
_____
_____
_____
_____
_____
_____
_____
_____
_____
_____
_____
_____
_____

Giddy

Impulsive, scatterbrain.
Online English Dictionary

"Did he *really* like me? Was I *too* short? Will he call?" Such questions employed my thoughts following a blind date. I was *giddy*– from emotional intoxication. Something happens when estrogen and testosterone collide.

"Where is he spiritually?" A good friend asked.

"He goes to church." I replied defensively. "When he's not playing golf on Sundays," I mentally concluded. "Oh, yes and his father is a minister," I tossed in. We both knew that there are many "Christians" with varying moral standards and many would not blink at the thought of fornication. It is somehow justifiable in their minds- he was one of them.

"Uh huh." She contemplated.

"Jeri." She spoke shattering the silence. "You deserve someone spiritually stable; who loves the Lord not someone you will have to carry spiritually..." her words buzzed in the air like swarming bees; but I knew she was speaking the truth.

I was confounded at how far I had strayed in such short time. Rather than actively pursuing God I was yielding to the spirit of loneliness. My glamorized perception of him camouflaged our apparent incompatibilities. My scattered focus allowed my passions to arise and strangle me. Two weeks later the Holy Spirit was *finally* able to get through.

I was flirting with a situation fertile for breeding disappointment, pain, fornication and remorse. My friend had the spiritual insight to see this and the courage to warn me. I said good-bye to this handsome distraction. Thank God, for re-focusing me. With renewed commitment and a cleared mind, I pledged to *wait* for God to send the person who is right for me.

> Be self-controlled and alert. Your enemy the devil prowls
> around like a roaring lion looking
> for someone to devour.
> I Peter 5:7-9

Thoughts

How do you ground your emotions when feeling giddy in the presence of you are attracted to?

_____
_____
_____
_____
_____
_____
_____
_____
_____
_____
_____
_____
_____
_____
_____
_____
_____
_____
_____
_____

Moses

**"What if what we see isn't the truth, and only
color-blind people see what's really there?"
Anonymous**

Moses chose to marry a Cushite woman while serving his father-in-law in the desert. This caused conflict with his brother and sister and they spoke out against the interracial marriage- big mistake! God reacted by allowing his sister, Miriam to experience a condition called Leprosy. After Moses prayed her condition was healed; but Miriam had to remain outside the camp for seven days according to customs. This story makes it clear that God is concerned with our heart- not the color of our skin. Even today, many are not able to move beyond skin color.

"I would never marry outside my race," I have heard this in group conversations with other women. I don't think these results are rooted in racism; but rather a defining of personal preferences and comfort zones. It's sad if two people with the important things in life in common let color be the only dividing factor. Some of the most beautiful couples I've met are interracial. It takes both courage and compromise. Courage to profess love for one another in a country that can be hostile and loaded with racial tensions. It takes compromises and agreeing to learn, accept and respect each other's ethnic differences.

It's important for couples to achieve mutual agreements on how to deal with developing and merging their cultural lifestyles. A Christian engaged to someone who wants polygamous lifestyle or worships other gods is not practical. A woman who has learned to be self-sufficient would not want to unite with someone who views women as subservient homemakers. Being equally yoked to someone who loves you and loves God is important—*really* important. Moreso, than color.

*He brought me to his special large room for eating,
and his colors over me were love.
Song of Solomon 2:4 NIV*

Thoughts

Would you marry someone of a different ethnicity and culture than yours?

Song

**One is taught by experience to put a premium on people
who can appreciate you for what you are.**
Gail Godwin

It's taken years to summon enough courage to become receptive to the idea of marriage *again.* I have been single for a *lo—nnnng* time. I've said I desired marriage in the past— usually not with *total* sincerity. These longings often arose when taking out the trash or bringing in the groceries and thoughts of *how nice it would be to have someone to share daily mundane tasks* that emerge. Like a rosebud my heart is expanding and entertaining possibilities of a *healthy* relationship.

I'm developing *my* voice as a single person. Even when younger the thought of dating can cause anxiety and questions about how you should respond. Such emotions intensify with age. It's important to flow from an *authentic* place while exchanging the verbal melodies necessary to *really* get to know someone.

The amazing chemistry between men and women creates a mind-altering attraction. I don't want to communicate in an *artificial-giddy-emotionally-intoxicated-school girlish frame of mind—* though it happens! My life is a song, and I am constantly searching for the right key. Once found I can rest assured that those in my audience are there because they enjoy— *my* song.

You who dwell in the gardens with friends in attendance,
let me hear your voice!
Song of Solomon 8:13 NIV

Thoughts

What type of song do others hear released through your life? One of joy or hopelessness? Sorrow or expectation? Other?

_____
_____
_____
_____
_____
_____
_____
_____
_____
_____
_____
_____
_____
_____
_____
_____
_____
_____
_____
_____

Boobs

"I hope people realise that there is a brain underneath the hair and a heart underneath the boobs."
Dolly Parton

During my tween years I recall swiping my mom's bra and stuffing it with socks and proudly parading the playground afterschool. Others eyed my overnight endowment with knowing suspicion. This memory resurfaced while watching a TV show. "The Bank of Hollywood" It aired people pitching proposals to celebrities in effort to convince them to finance their dreams. The range of request went from heart wrenching to bizarre. A woman sporting a busty figure who was the mother of an eighteen-year-old made a request for money for breast implants for her daughter.

This mother explained how breast implants boosted her confidence and self-esteem and she was requesting eighteen thousand dollars to provide her daughter with the same modifications to lift her confidence. The eighteen-year-old was introduced and had obviously small breast. One of the younger female celebrities attempted to reason with the daughter by sharing that her breast grew suddenly after she turned seventeen. Another celebrity owned a successful modeling agency and informed her that many models had breast even smaller than hers.

Their words of wisdom failed to penetrate the ingrained perception that beauty and boobs were equivalent. The request was denied-Thank God! The eighteen-year-old and mom walked away determined to find other means to achieve their goal. Surgical alteration of a yet developing human body—not wise! Too many women look like mannequins and some have died from complications of surgical modifications. This is sad. God thank you for loving us just as we are. Lord, please help us to love ourselves...

The Lord does not look at the things people look at. People look at the outward appearance, but the Lord looks at the heart.
I Samuel 16:7 NIV

Thoughts

What do think about the extent people are willing to go to surgically alter their appearance?

Integrity

**Live so that when your children think of fairness,
caring, and integrity, they think of you.
H. Jackson Brown, Jr.**

A clerk owed me eleven dollars, but gave me three, crisp five-dollar bills. I returned them, and she thanked me. Then I awoke to discover I was dreaming. Just like in the dream, Store clerks and bank tellers have erred in my favor- for much more than a few dollars. God gives me grace to respond with integrity. I was tested again when cashing an income tax check.

I signed my check at the drive-through window. "We cannot give this amount at the window," the teller explained. I parked and went inside and was handed sixteen-hundred dollars in hundred-dollar bills. I drove home and while putting my money away I discovered my unstamped check along with the bank's copy of the deposit slip.

Of course, this was a time when money was scarce and needs plentiful. I stared at the money and check wondering, "Why me?" I tried calling the bank' but the phone was busy. With fifteen minutes before closing I dashed out. The teller looked confused while I attempted to explain. Finally, I gave her the check saying, "I just needed to return this." I drove away feeling victorious. Being single with one income, no sugar daddy and mounting bills, I certainly could have used the extra cash. I believe in doing the right thing.

"Integrity is when you do the right thing, even when no one is watching," is how I explained it to my adolescent son who was *certain* this was God's blessing. I try to live with integrity, but I'm not always this successful. It's usually the *"little things"* that snare me. Only- what does God consider a "little thing?"

*The blessing of the Lord, it maketh rich, and
He addedth no sorrow with it.
Proverbs 10:22KJV*

Thoughts

Write about a significant act of integrity done on your part.

My Confession

Life
Has taught me
That I am strong.
In fact
I am stronger
Than
I
Think I am.
I am as strong as I
Need to be.
When I am Weak
I
Am Strong.
His strength is perfect
When my strength is
Gone.

Thoughts

Write a personal confession for your life.

Liars!

**You can bend it and twist it... You can misuse and abuse it...
But even God cannot change the Truth."
Michael Levy**

"I like your hair." Thanks, I smiled.

"My fifth grade son is growing into such a considerate young man—"*I thought.*

"I like your hair." Then I noticed him snickering as he showered *every* female he encountered with this same compliment. Teachers, parents, secretaries—didn't matter. Still didn't think much of this—until—"I like your hair."

It was during a parent's conference—I looked into the face of his aging teacher with bald spots peering through the short scanty strands of gray hair scattered atop of her head. She looked embarrassed knowing his words lacked sincerity. Then I knew—we had to talk. He was geeked by the ability of his words to evoke a notable change in women. Smiles, vulnerability followed this simple praise from a male *child*—whether or not it was genuine. Imagine the impact of flattering words from a man or woman planted into a lonely heart.

We talked—I tried *hard* to impress upon him the difference in compliments, flattery and outright *lying*! Hope he internalized it! Many relationships are built upon slippery slopes of flattery and lies. When such behaviors are repeated over the years they become communication norms. One is hardly conscious of the fact that they are outright—*lying.*

A sincere compliment radiates the spirit and infuses the receiver with joy. Relationships built upon such can become strong towers. Don't know about you—but if I can't trust one to be honest about my hair— that one will *not* be trusted with my heart. Come on! Women...*men too*; let's not be *that* gullible!

**Let no man deceive you with vain words:
Ephesians 5:6 KJV**

Thoughts

Can you tell if someone is attempting to deceive you with vain words?

Signals

*If a woman driver ahead of you signals a left turn,
be careful, she may turn left.*
James Thurber

"You're not going? "My friend and I went two nights to a local revival. We planned to attend the third. I drove as she did not have transportation- but I decided not to go. I cannot always keep the pace of even those closest to me. I strive to allow the Holy Spirit to direct how I flow through the traffic of this life. Thank God, He did make a way for her to attend. Finding the right rhythm, pace and direction is an ongoing saga. Like automobiles from all directions meeting at an intersection and each driver is governed by the light signal they are directly facing.

From the four corners of the earth; God's people are looking to Him for direction. Countless prayers and petitions constantly ascend before Him, yet He gives each individual signals to order our steps. Some are directed to stop- *immediately!* Others warned to slow down and proceed with caution. Then others get green light- go! My favorite is when He gives a green arrow signaling to turn while He holds back opposing forces from all directions. This signal alerts that it is safe to alter your course when life is presenting new opportunities or necessary changes.

Traveling companions are great but sometimes we are directed in opposing directions. When God's signals are ignored, and everyone follows their own inclination it causes chaos resulting in casualties. Watch for God's signals when allowing others in and out of your life. When attuned to His divine signals, we are assured of arriving at our divine destinations safe and at the appointed time with the right people.

I will instruct thee and teach thee in the way which thou shalt go: I will guide thee with mine eye.
Psalm 32:8 KJV

Thoughts

Have you felt that God was leading you in a different direction from someone close to you?

Who?

If you want to forget something or someone, never hate it, or never hate him/her. Everything and everyone that you hate is engraved upon your heart; if you want to let go of something, if you want to forget, you cannot hate."
C. JoyBell C

"God, how long will my mind be tormented by thoughts of— *him?*" I prayed seeing no soon end to my emotional anguish.

"Let me pray for you." A friend and confidante requested after I shared news of my *slow* emotional recovery. With much love and compassion—she prayed. I awoke the next morning expecting to be haunted by the emptiness and disenchantment resulting from abandonment. The sad and anguished feelings that had stalked me for weeks had-vanished! This emotional recuperation was just as miraculous as any physical healing.

God revived my heart and emotions while I slept. I arose— completely *whole!* How are you doing?" My friend asked a few days later. I knew she was referring to my recent emotional suffering. She thought I was joking when I had difficulty recalling his name! It's unbelievable to me!

"No. *Really*, I can't remember his name," I insisted. I did later that day with much mental effort. To this day I have trouble recalling his name. Not only did God destroy the soul tie, but He erased the counterfeit imprints from my heart that I mistook for love. I was *fully* restored to pre-heartbreak status. Our God is simply amazing- isn't He?

The LORD is high above all nations, and his glory above the heavens. Who is like unto the LORD our God, who dwelleth on high?
Psalm 113:4, 5 KJV

Thoughts

Have you released emotional pain from a past relationship or relationships?

Standards

"I'm tired, fed up with trying to fit into somebody else's standards,"
David Burke

I attended a meeting with a panel of men of various ages. Most were in marriages ranging from 6 to 35 years. A couple were single. They were requested to answer questions about men posed by an audience of single women. One woman asked, "Why is it that when a man cheats in most cases the woman is able to eventually to forgive and move on. When a woman cheats the man never forgets and continually brings it up when he's angry?"

"For women it is a heart issue, but for men it is a matter of pride." Decent response I thought.

"What do you think?" I asked a male friend later that night. After a long hesitation he said.

"Men hold women to a higher standard. I know it is not fair, but it's true. You remember how we responded as children when someone talked about our mothers?" Interesting perspective. I am thankful that the standards that God holds for both men and women are not gender biased. Society has always been quick to throw stones at women for sexual indiscretions and being less judgmental when dealing with men.

"Boys will be boys." The cliché' goes. I'm glad that God does not have double standards. What's good for the gander is good for the goose! I know I wrote that cliché' backwards:)

When the enemy shall come in like a flood, the Spirit of the LORD shall lift up a standard against him.
Isaiah 59:19 KJV

Thoughts

Give an example of how you have witnessed women measured by different standards than men?

Query

**A question that you ask because you want information or because
you are not certain about something
Macmillan Dictionary**

"God, am I a good Christian?" I flung this query at Him. Of course, I could pray more, read my Bible more, be more patient, kinder, gentler, *more*..." I sighed while summing up the measure of a *good* Christian in my mind. God has unique ways of responding to such ponderings. A friend that I'd been out of touch with for a year and a half came to mind again. I thought about her over the past several months and never phoned. I searched diligently for her number and located it just before giving up. "Hello!" I greeted.

"Je-ri!!! It's good to hear from you. God is so awesome! I just hung up the phone. I called The 700 Club for prayer and asked God to bring Christians into my life. I was specific-I asked for '*good*' Christians. I didn't expect Him to answer *tha-at* quickly..."

She agreed to attend a revival with me and I arranged a time to pick her up. My heart filled with compassion watching her slowly descend the steps with a cane. I was unaware that she had suffered a stroke. As I drove she updated me on her physical and personal challenges. Her eyes shone with hope and her words were charged with faith. I was thankful that I responded to God's prompt to call her. It proved to be a blessing for us both.

"Thank You Lord." I thought. "I go through the motions of trying to do the right thing. With all my heart I desire to please God. I am not a *perfect* Christian, but I do attempt to be a *good* one." With His help I will succeed in this endeavor.

**So for a whole year Barnabas and Saul met with the church and taught great
numbers of people. The disciples were called
Christians first at Antioch.
Acts 11:26 NLT**

Thoughts

What do you consider qualities of a "good Christian?" Do you see them in your life?

Circulation

How can God direct our steps if we're not taking any?
Sarah Leah Grafsten

Stagnation breed boredom, boredom breeds frustration, and frustration, anger, and anger fear, and fear despair, and despair, hopelessness, and hopelessness, defeat. If life feels stagnant- check your circulation! A life of purposeful movement! That's my innermost desire. Conquering unknown terrains, engaging in enriching life experiences, connecting with stimulating people- it's the circulation of life! The human heart demonstrates the importance of circulation.

The heart's pumping propels all that's vital throughout the body. When the heart stops, blood pools and stagnates—within minutes—life ceases. Keep *moving*! It's important especially as seasoned single Christians. No, not desperate, calculated efforts to maneuver into *right* places- at *right* times, attempting to connect with perfect partners. Circulate with the Holy Spirit in and out of rich arteries of invigorating experiences.

Defy stagnation by purposeful exploration of God's word. Explore the universe with active pursuit of His purpose— for you! It is not too late to access veins crammed with promise of wealthy experiences. Such movement accelerates interpersonal growth and spiritual depth. Want to blaze through this single's journey leaving a trail of fond, invigorating memories? You can do it! Keep circulating!

For in him we live and move and have our being...
Acts 17:28 KJV

Thoughts

Identify and write about new areas you can explore to avoid feeling stagnant?

Accepted

**Be who you are and say what you mean, those that mind don't matter,
and those that matter don't mind.**
Dr. Seuss

Her shoulders shook as sobs erupted from deep within. Sadness filled the room like thick smoke. "He looks at me with such disgust! I feel like he is only tolerating my presence!" This woman was referring to a leader in her church. She felt rejection when in his presence.

Problems occur when we become emotionally crippled when others cause us to feel unaccepted. You may offer the world your best and yet for some this will *never* be good enough. The question is do you change while attempting to please them—or continue being yourself? It takes courage to walk in your authentic uniqueness revealing your true self to the world whether others like it or not.

It is human nature to desire to be respected and accepted by others. We all want to fit in—somewhere. Rejection can be rooted in childhood or occur when older. Trauma from relationship breakups, exclusion from church clichés or emotional wounds from the past can cause feelings of rejection. These bitter emotions are not always easy to shake off. If not addressed, they will stunt your growth. Start by developing a healthy opinion of yourself and learning to value *it* above the opinions of others.

People are too numerous and diverse to gear our lives towards pleasing them *all!* There will *always* be some who just don't get you. Don't compromise the integrity of your inner being by struggling to receive their acceptance. Just the way you are—Jesus loves and has *already* accepted you. It's okay—be *YOU.* He will *never* laugh, criticize or reject you in any way for any reason. If you have not accepted Him, you *can* do so *RIGHT NOW.*

To the praise of the glory of his grace, wherein
he hath made us accepted in the beloved.
Ephesians 1:6 KJV

Thoughts

How do you handle it when you feel someone has rejected you?

Might

Strength or ability to do something
American Heritage Dictionary

"Mom!" you should have seen that bird!" My 17-year-old son exclaimed. It was flapping its wings and not getting anywhere! It was almost upside down!" I can relate to this, on this day the winds were so ferocious winds that I had to cut through them using the force of my body weight.

This bird illustrates what it's like facing life's opposition in *our own strength*. As we grow older we may become more determined to be impactful. Our futile efforts fail to propel us forward. This can be discouraging. Many people feel unseen forces are holding them back and preventing them from achieving their dreams. So did I when I limited myself to my finite energies.

Even though we are seasoned *and* single we don't face life's adversity alone. We *can* rely on God's strength. Knowing this gives me the confidence, courage and determination to forge through life's battles. I walk with the One who commands the wind, moves mountains and empowers me to do all things through Him. (Philippians 4:13) And so do you...

"...Not by might, nor by power, but by my Spirit, saith the Lord of hosts."
Zechariah 4:6 KJV

Thoughts

How do you know when you are operating in your own strength rather than God's?

Impeccable

*It is only with the heart that one can see rightly;
what is essential is invisible to the eye.*
Antoine de Saint Exupéry

Walking in the mall I passed a woman with such a polished look! Stylish hair, tailored clothing, tasteful make-up and carefully manicured hands and toenails- she was *impeccable!* It was evident that her appearance was not at the bottom of her priorities and she invested quality time. I admired her!

It provoked me—for a season to get on the ball. I get by with my outward preparation. It's acceptable. I get a fair share of compliments—*but* I certainly could pay greater attention to details. I would love to be one of those *"not-a-hair-out-of-place"* women. How does one find the time?

As a single seasoned woman; I find that I feel better and interact with the world with increased confidence when I invest time into *putting myself together.* Sometimes when singles take time to get spiffy others will give you the twice over and will ask, "Are you seeing someone?" Like you do not value yourself to look your best—just for youself. It is okay to be impeccable, just because, just for you. Because you are sons and daughters of a Great King who *so* loves you.

God is more concerned with the inner adornment of our spirit. Though impeccable on the outside many are betrayed with speech and actions. The unattractiveness of their character and spirit blurs the outer presentation. As I work on improving my outward appearance my greater priority is presenting to God an *impeccable heart.* But hey, it is okay to be impeccable inside and out! *Right?*

Whose adorning let it not be that outward adorning of plaiting the hair, and of wearing of gold, or of putting on of apparel; 'But let it be the hidden man of the heart, in that which is not corruptible, even the ornament of a meek and quiet spirit, which is in the sight of God of great price.
1 Peter 3:3,4 KJV

Thoughts

Are there areas that you would like to be more consistent when it comes to your appearance? What heart issues would you like to be more impeccable?

_____
_____
_____
_____
_____
_____
_____
_____
_____
_____
_____
_____
_____
_____
_____
_____
_____
_____

Spice

Something that adds zest or flavor.
American Heritage Online Dictionary

After being single for many years I befriended a man who lived in another city. We had phone conversations. He was talkative, knowledgeable and respectful. I'm naturally shy; but our talks taught me to keep talking even when my words threatened to shrivel and vanish mid-sentence. It was a growing experience. Many during their seasoned years' experience the awkwardness of a teenager when chatting with the opposite sex.

I struggled with freezing up when communicating with boys even when young. I was *clueless* how to respond when a man expressed an interest in me even as an adult. I struggle for words; but they remain locked inside. Progress in interacting with men has been slow over the years- otherwise I consider myself to be an excellent communicator. This gentleman helped me to breakthrough this tongue-tied stage.

"He's boring, I concluded after hanging up the phone one night.

"Why should he be totally responsible for an interesting conversation?" I was startled and challenged by this question in my mind— Yep, I had shouldered him with the duty of injecting excitement into our talks. I began spicing up our talks by taking conversational risks. I introduced topics that would have normally remained unspoken. This caused him to stretch and our conversations ascended to new levels. Enjoyable levels. They were transformed into a pleasant rather than a dreary experience. No, we were not a love connection— but we both obtained insight into the art of spicy, yet wholesome conversation.

> Let your speech *be* always with grace, seasoned with salt, that ye may know how ye ought to answer every man.
> Colossians 4:6 KJV

Thoughts

Do you become tongue tied when someone express an interest in getting to know you?

_____
_____
_____
_____
_____
_____
_____
_____
_____
_____
_____
_____
_____
_____
_____
_____
_____
_____
_____
_____

Thoughts

What crosses your mind when you consider that God knew you before you were born?

Issues

"You all have issues but don't make peace with them."
Unknown

"At age 8 she struggled with *issues* of self-esteem." I said while reading a story I'd written about one of my granddaughters, to all four of my grandchildren. The story highlighted her willingness to shower her siblings with praise during a game. "What did you think? I asked when finished. A perplexed expression covered her face. "What's wrong?"

"You said I have *issues!* She pronounced frowning with displeasure.

"What does that mean to you?" She had zoned in on this one word so intensely that I don't thing think she heard another word of my glowing commendations aimed at encouraging her.

"It means, I'm *crazy* or something!" *"Issues,"* even at this early age, she knew that whatever they were— they were undesirable, and she didn't want any.

"No sweetheart, *everyone* has issues," I explained. It's true. The woman in the scriptures had an issue with blood for eighteen years. Though this was an actual physical condition for her; the word *"blood"* in the Bible is often interchangeable with the word *"life."*

Nobody wants issues; but satan makes sure we *all* have them. Over the years our accumulation of issues can become enormous. If you are fortunate; they will cause you to pursue the Living God. Whether physical, emotional or spiritual- whether we are single, married or divorced- we shall *all* encounter issues along the way. Regardless of our issues or how long we have struggled with them, *Jesus is the answer.* You can reach out and touch Him- with any and all issues that concern you—reach out *today.*

And, behold, a woman, which was diseased with an issue of blood twelve years, came behind him, and touched the hem of his garment.
Matthew 9:2 KJV

Thoughts

Do you have an unresolved issue that has plagued you for (too many) years?

_____
_____
_____
_____
_____
_____
_____
_____
_____
_____
_____
_____
_____
_____
_____
_____
_____
_____
_____
_____
_____
_____

O*n*line.com

People do and say things online that they would never do otherwise. The people I see in my office- they're not perverts, but they get online and suddenly, they're sex fiends."
David Greenfield

Meet your *perfect* match—online ads bombarded my laptop. I declined random invites; convinced these sites harbored weird, desperate people. One day— curiosity won and I completed the *"free"* guest registration. Chat invites started immediately. A chat opened with a reminder that I was *just a guest* urging me to upgrade- for a modest fee (of course). I declined!

Another chat invite ignited my overactive imagination. Curious, I clicked to upgrade my account. I laughed while reading an invite from a twenty-year-old in Nigeria. "Too young," I replied. Seconds later I read his updated profile- he'd aged to forty in seconds! Deceit, disillusion and danger are realities of online dating. Just like meeting people in *any* environment. Yet there are many irrefutable success stories such as that of a friend who met her marital match online. They are stilled happily married.

The online dating is an option that many are choosing to meet others. A woman said, "my pastor forbids it!" That's a lot of control to give to a pastor in my estimation. Is it safe? That depends on the maturity and safety practices observed. If freshly wounded, desperate, co-dependent, naïve or overeager to dive into a relationship—you might want to wait until you achieve some emotional stability.

Review warnings and suggestions offered about online meetings. I don't promote or diss online relationships. It depends on the individual. Being led by wounded emotions is not the best way to proceed with online or any other type of relationship. What's most important knowing God's voice *and* following Him. If you are online or thinking about it—seek wisdom, read the warnings and proceed with caution. It's a new day!

If any of you lacks wisdom, you should ask God who gives generously to all without finding fault, and it will be given to you.
James 1:5 NIV

Thoughts

What pros and cons come to your mind about online dating?

HTN

"They waste their whole day, so they won't go unless they are really sick. Some People coming into the hospital are dying. They didn't know they had high blood pressure and already had a stroke. They just come in to die."
Nop Ratanasiripong

Following a back injury my employer insisted that I see a doctor. Elevated blood pressure! Couldn't believe it! My blood pressure was normally great, I was feeling the best ever! Memories of romantic stories about people who prayed for a relationship and met a wonderful person. Their *brief*, beautiful marriage- cut short by premature death. High blood pressure can result in sudden stroke, aneurysms or other serious medical conditions—including death. It is treatable and should **NEVER** be ignored.

I do blood pressure clinics for the community and it is not uncommon for about 80% them to have abnormal readings. This disorder tends to run in families. Both my parents and seven siblings were all diagnosed. Two brothers had open heart surgery—twice. A younger sister experienced an aneurysm and multiple strokes. While watching TV with family, a brother slipped into a coma from an aneurysm. They thought he was asleep; he died within several days.

This *symptomless* disorder is easy to ignore. Unemployment and lack of health insurance results in many not seeking treatment. There are resources in most communities. Your local Red Cross or health department is a good place to begin research. Health insurance—or not—go to the emergency room if your blood pressure is dangerously high and you do not know what else to do.

I'm a believer in divine healing and have received physical miracles through prayer over the years. But I advocate medical evaluation and treatment *with* medications- while praying. Take care of yourself for yourself and your future life partner. You both deserve it!

Beloved, I wish above all things that you prosper and be in health even as your soul prospers.
3 John 3:2 KJV

Thoughts

Are you ignoring physical symptoms that you know should be discussed with a doctor? If so, schedule your appointment TODAY.

Gossip

Gossip needn't to be false to be evil- there's a lot of truth that shouldn't be passed around.
Frank A. Clark

A friend shared frustration with a relative. "She goes from house-to-house passing people business. I shared something with her and emphasized—*don't* share this with *anyone*!" She agreed. "The next thing I knew she was right back over repeating the very same story to me full of inaccurate details!"

Then said, "I can't remember who told me this." I listened with a look of astonishment! Speechless! Didn't bother to inform her that I was the original source."

"That's funny!" Snickering and struggling not to laugh. Gossip is *no* laughing matter. Gossipers are easily recognized. They gravitate toward lower level conversations focused on people rather than goals, vision or purpose. They are not interested in your pain- nor your cure—just your tale. They thrust baited questions like pros and reel in juicy details capturing your secrets. They leave with your scoop—eager to share their prize catch!

Many seasoned singles stuffed years of emotional pain attempting to escape gossip. Who can you trust in this "*need to know-gotta tell*" age? Those with healthy marital relationships have someone to share the joys, pains and traumas of this life. If fortunate, singles have family, friends or other supportive relationships in which to confide. Not every marriage is healthy and not every single is fortunate.

Though many despise gossip, it is contagious. If you have been infected, God has the cure. Ask him to teach you to set a guard to your lips. He will. There is no need to leak every morsel or tidbit of information you hear about someone. Everyone needs a *trustworthy* person to talk with in dark seasons. Are you *trustworthy?* If not, why not? You only please satan with gossip.

He that goes about as a talebearer reveals secrets,
But he that is trustworthy conceals a matter.
Proverbs 11:13 KJV

Thoughts

Does fear of gossip hinder you from sharing problems and feelings that you REALLY would like to talk about?

Impasse

"A situation in which progress is not possible because none of the people involved are willing to change their opinion or decision."
Macmillan Online Dictionary

"Hi Sweetie," I overheard a man's phone greeting which jolted my mind to a recent relationship. The attraction was like a whirlwind from inception filled with exhilarating conversations. There were seasons when the impact of twisting through differences and misunderstandings felt overwhelming. Hours invested into chatting and phone conversations revealed many compatibilities. It was like something beautiful blossoming. We were exploring possibilities of a joint future.

We clashed sometimes; but always managed to guide one another back onto a path of mutual respect, understanding and forgiveness. "Let's continue this process of discovery," he'd challenge. We did... until—the deadlock...the **sex before marriage** impasse. The place where many relationships crash and burn!

Both unwilling to compromise; our communications fizzled like the last beads of water evaporating from a boiling pot. "My desire and intent to remain abstinent until marriage is non-negotiable." I reiterated in closing chat. You would have thought he was hearing this for the first time, though it was on the table from the get-go.

"THIS IS INSANE!! To think that any attraction that you have to me would threaten your standing with God! This process of discovery is *over!"* His exiting words was like the forceful slamming of a door leaving a haunting echo. Though my heart ached, I felt God's reassuring voice, "If you only knew the heartbreak that I have just spared you- you would rejoice! *I believe Him.*

"...and what he shuts no one can open."
Revelation 3:7 KJV

Thoughts

Write about your recovery from an emotional wreck, following any sort of relationship problem.

Jealousy

Jealousy lives upon doubts. It becomes madness or ceases entirely as soon as we pass from doubt to certainty.
Francois de La Rochefoucauld

Locate jealousy in your body—a devotional piece ended on this note. I shared this reading with a co-worker. At first, she shrugged her shoulders. Then looking into my eyes admitted, "you know, sometimes I *do* feel jealous. When I see a couple together, I ask myself, *why* can't that be me? I never thought of it as jealousy before, but that's what it is..." What honesty!

Seeing couples who *look* happy can trigger or intensify longings for a husband or a wife. Some of us have been alone for years. We are human, jealousy can and will arise. It is a work of the flesh in which our spirit resides. It only festers if allowed to linger. Though it happens; it need not become toxic. Jealousy is overridden by the continual renewal of our minds and recognizing the bridge between normal healthy admiration and jealousy.

The Holy Spirit's purpose is to comfort, support, strengthen and guide us with staying on course while waiting for the desire of meeting someone special to manifest—if that's God's plan. Be truthful when talking to God about any thoughts, emotions or fears that arises during this journey- *whatever* they might be—including jealousy. You can be *completely* honest with Him. You're *not* alone with juggling wavering emotions—of any sort.

But I trust in your unfailing love; my heart rejoices in your salvation. I will sing to the Lord, for he has been good to me.
Psalm 13:5-6 NLT

Thoughts

Are you honest with God (and yourself) when sharing emotions that sometimes arise when surrounded by couples?

Knowledge

Knowledge is power.
Francis Bacon

I was watching a TV show and there was a woman looking in the mirror wearing a *perfectly fitting black dress.* Ironically, at that very moment I was looking in my mirror wearing a *perfectly fitting black dress*— after losing fifty pounds and four dress sizes. It was surreal. After adapting a new way of eating and losing fifty pounds in six months—I *was* elated! Eight months after this victory I had gained twenty-eight of them back and a few months later the entire fifty making the earlier victory seemed like an elusive dream.

Not again! I thought looking in the mirror with unmerciful frustration. This same week I visited the doctor who was treating me for back strain. "Everything looks good, keep doing your back exercises..." He lingered, and we talked about several topics— including weight. The doctor shared his tactics for maintaining a slim, muscular frame. He spoke with passion and concern.

"I lost fifty pounds on a diet, I mean life maintenance plan." I try to avoid the term *"diet."* The friendly physician smiled realizing that I already possessed sufficient knowledge and needed only to act on it.

He said, "You will lose the weight, you *know* what to do." His words etched in my head and reverberated all that day. The doctor was right. There was a time when I struggled with my weight and didn't have a clue what to do. Today—I knew and just need to utilize the tools I possess. Whatever our struggles God has solutions. Hearing His wisdom and knowledge and failing to act is useless. It's true, knowledge without action is worthless.

Be ye doers of the word, and not a hearer of only,
deceiving your own selves.
James 1:22 KJV

Thoughts

Name and explain one thing that you want to change and have knowledge (that you are not using) to overcome.

Murmuring

*Man spends his life in reasoning on the past, in complaining
of the present, in fearing future.*
Antoine Rivarol

"That will be forty-nine, thirty-five" the teller announced with a perky smile. It was payday, I stopped by the store with the intentions of spending a "*few*" dollars.

While passing my debit card, I sighed thinking, "God, I'm tired of constantly stretching my check which is *too small* to begin with!" My negative mental rantings were ready to erupt full-force when I sensed these words inside.

"Have you missed a meal?"

"No, Lord, I haven't."

"Have you missed paying a bill?" The questioning continued.

"No, Lord, I haven't."

"Aren't you driving a new company car that you drove out of the showroom and don't have to pay for?"

"Yes, Lord."

"Then why don't you thank Me?" While dropping the sales receipt in my purse and walking out of the store my mind flooded with account after of account of God's faithful provision.

"I'm so sorry;" I repented recognizing that I am guilty of taking for granted the daily onslaught of God's blessings. I had allowed the enemy to prod me toward murmuring and dissatisfaction. "No more!" I decided, I couldn't think of *any* reason why I should be doing anything *except* praising God for His goodness.

Living single and shouldering life's responsibility can give way to feelings of frustration. The enemy can cloud our thinking until we tend to only see dark clouds rather than the light of God's Son shining upon us.

*Rejoice always, pray without ceasing, give thanks in all circumstances;
for this is the will of God in Christ Jesus for you.*
1 Thessalonians 5:16-18 NIV

Thoughts

Start a gratitude list. Use each line to list what you are grateful for during this season of your life.

Chosen

"All our young lives we search for someone to love. We choose partners, change partners... all the while wondering if there's someone, somewhere, searching for us."
Anonymous

Were you ever left standing after teams were chosen as a child? Have you silently prayed that *someone, anyone* would ask you to dance? Proms, dating going steady—intimidating milestones for both males and females. Even in our youth we had no desire watch others while we stood alone on the sidelines—unchosen. Being chosen is critical to our esteem and feeling social acceptance. Women were once taught that it is proper to *wait* for the man to approach first. Things have changed much over the years.

Men were once taught to pursue a woman if interested. Yet many men are terrified of pursing a woman that peaked their interest. Some men feel that women fail to communicate clearly that they are receptive and this results in hesitation. He may never risk exploring if the feeling is mutual for fear of being—*unchosen*. As he fades into the background the woman is often left clueless.

You read books, attended conferences and allowed God to make crooked places straight where change was needed. Each passing birthday can cause the battle against fears of being overlooked to increase. Diabolic whisperings may construct self-blame for prolonged singleness. It takes utilizing spiritual strategies to silence the negative voices and allow God to comfort and strengthen us during these seasons.

Jesus is acquainted with grief and experiences the rejection of being unchosen daily. Rejected by those that He loved to the point of self-sacrifice. God's love sustains me. It gives me victory over mental warfare knowing that I am chosen and loved by Him the giver of life and the answerer of prayers.

Ye have not chosen me, but I have chosen you, and ordained you, that ye should go and bring forth fruit, and that your fruit should remain: that whatsoever ye shall ask of the Father in my name, he may give it you.
John 15:16 KJV

Thoughts

Write a note to God, thanking Him for choosing "YOU." For loving "YOU."

Despair

You are as young as your self-confidence, as old as your fears;
as young as your hope as old as your despair.
Samuel Ulman

Leaving work, I was indecisive about what fast food restaurant to choose for a quick bite. When attempting to check the voicemail from my cell phone, my call was redirected to customer service. "God, I am tired," I thought feeling financially frustrated. I waited for someone to assist me with my call.

While wallowing in frustration I grabbed my debit card to pay the bill. "Turn your phone off and back on and your service will be restored." The customer service rep instructed after providing my confirmation number. I left the fast food drive-through feeling relieved to have a functioning cell phone once again. Though that was taken care of, a lingering sense of despair clung, and I silently communicated this to God.

While doing so my eyes absorbed the image of an aged woman on the sidewalk. I assessed her emotional state while driving past. Her aged appearance was not a result of birthdays. Perhaps she was sick or dabbling in drugs; but living in a state of perpetual despair likely played a role.

"That is the face of despair," The Lord clarified. My earlier frustrations melted. I realized that instead of throwing tantrums for minor inconveniences which readily resolved by tapping a few buttons; I could be sharing His Goodness with those experiencing *real* despair. Let's take a moment to pray for those who are in despair; for whatever reason. Ask God how you can help Him to encourage others.

The harvest truly is plenteous; but the laborers are few..
Mathew 9:37 KJV

Thoughts

Think of someone who is experiencing despair (greater than yours) and write a prayer for them.

Brighter Days

Thoughts

Describe on lines below what your "brighter days" will look like.

Connecting

*The more social media we have, them more we think we're connecting, yet we are
Really disconnecting from each other.*
JR

The opposite of intimacy is distant. Just because you are standing next to a person and peering into their eyes doesn't mean you're connected. Living a distant life is all too familiar to me. My reluctant journey of connecting with others began with God nudging me out of my comfort zone. It's important to *REALLY* connect with others in a meaningful way. "I am *not* a people person." I proclaimed this over my life for years.

"Stop saying that!" God urged. "You *are* a person, I made you a people person." My obedience has resulted in some amazing connections over this year. My only regret is that it took me so long to listen and began connecting with others. We miss out on much in life when we allow our pain, fear or shyness to avoid the pleasure of sharing our life's journey with others. It saddens me when I consider how long it took me to venture out; yet I am excited that the expedition has begun!

I still have a longways to go; but I'm on my way! If you have failed to connect with others over the course of your life— join me on this exciting venture. It takes courage and intentional effort to be present, to ***connect—for real***. Start today! Call, inbox, text or messenger someone that you have desired to connect with but didn't for whatever reason. I kept list of people to connect with and allowed years to pass without ever reaching out to them.

Several awesome women lingered on my *someday* list. One by one they each died from terminal illnesses. I felt cheated, deprived of any precious moments I could have shared with them. We don't have all the time in the world to connect with each other—we have *today*—we have *now!* If God leads you to connect with someone—*do it—NOW!*

He makes the whole body fit together perfectly. As each part does its own special work, it helps the other parts grow, so that the whole body is healthy and growing and full of love.
Ephesians 4:16 NLT

Thoughts

List three people that God has been leading you to connect with. Write about your hesitation then schedule a time to contact each one.

Laughter

A good time to laugh is any time you can.
Linda Ellerbee

Walking to my car while leaving the library I turned my head abruptly to give the young woman I had just passed a double-take. Her frame jiggled in laughter making her seem fully alive at that moment. The image of this woman lingered as I craved the healing properties of laughter to manifest in me once more. Genuine laughter like that gushing from the gut like a relentless volcanic eruption.

The past couple weeks life had me volleying in and out of despair. Real laughter seemed as unlikely as looking down and discovering a million dollars. It felt distant like something I read, dreamt, or perhaps saw in a movie. Trying not to stare I wondered, "God, will I *ever* laugh like *that-* again?" I couldn't perceive it.

Laughter, the kind that create body trembles, the kind swelling inside and contorting your mouth and facial muscles into weird expressions. Laughter, the kind that pierces the air and spreads joy like a contagious microbe-- How I missed it!

Desperation had narrowed my vision preventing me from seeing beyond the present disaster and overwhelming emotions. My mind hosted the pain of past failures, current realities and future doom while refusing to entertain the comfort that hope could offer. Satan had me convinced that I would *never* laugh again. He is such a liar! *Ha! Ha! Ha!*

A merry heart doeth good like a medicine: but a broken spirit drieth the bones.
Proverbs 17:22 KJV

Thoughts

Describe how you felt the last time you "REALLY" laughed.

_____
_____
_____
_____
_____
_____
_____
_____
_____
_____
_____
_____
_____
_____
_____
_____
_____
_____
_____
_____
_____
_____

Drudgery

Every worthwhile accomplishment, big or little, has its stages of drudgery and triumph; a beginning, a struggle and a victory.
Mahatma Gandhi

I drug in the house after ending a twelve-hour workday. I had every intention of eating and settling down to spend couple hours entering nursing assessments into the computer. I felt like I was betrothed to my job, connected to my computer and trapped in a ritual of mundane activities. Unloading the car, emptying the trash, checking the mailbox, making a meal, taking a bath, checking my email, and so on.

The past several years flashed before me replaying images of patterns of drudgery. There was a time that I forced myself to break such cycles venturing outside of routine realms. I took a class, conquered a fear or completed something on my goal list. Somehow my life had become unfocused, undisciplined, unpleasant, mundane and just plain boring!

"God, I don't want to live like this! Help me do something inciting." I prayed. It takes meaningful connections to break cycles of drudgery. It won't happen while cruising on automatic pilot and failing to really recognize when God brings along someone cross our path to break routines. Too often we pray for adventure and fail to receive others that are the door to something new.

Use your spiritual radar, recognize when God is presenting you with new people and new experiences. "Have a great day!" Allow God to do a new thing in you and--for you! Drudgery is not indestructible—it can be squashed, and your life revitalized with the power of the *NEW!*

Behold I will do a new thing; now shall it spring forth, shall ye not know it?
Isaiah 43:19 KJV

Thoughts

Start a list decreeing the "NEW" things you are believing God for in all areas of your life. Continue with more paper if needed.

_____
_____
_____
_____
_____
_____
_____
_____
_____
_____
_____
_____
_____
_____
_____
_____
_____
_____
_____

Retired?

I'm always announcing my retirement, I'm still not retired.
Dick Van Dyke

"Are you still working?" I get this from others from time to time. But one particular woman I can count on to ask *every* time our paths cross. "Are you still working?" These words rush from her lips before even saying hello! One day I saw her at a local store and sure enough, "Are you still working?" Was shouted from twenty feet away.

"*Why* do you ask me that **every** time you see me?" I finally asked.

She chuckled and said, "Because, I want you to be retired like me!" At least she was honest. I don't know what goes through a person's head when asking this question. Does it make them feel old because they are retired, and I am not? Do they pity me because they feel that I am too old to be working and should be retired? God only knows. We are each on individual and personal journeys while facing different realities.

When to retire is a private decision. The single life does not afford peace in knowing that there is a second income to rely upon when sick, for emergencies or even retirement. Many singles have exercised financial wisdom and are able to retire and live comfortably on one income. Working will be the reality for many while physically able. They may or may not be happy about this.

Though in my seasoned years, I am *still* working. Wishing I would have grasp the wisdom and courage to launch into entrepreneurship in earlier years. Looking back with regret has no real value. Moving forward armed with the lessons of the past is priceless. I'm grasping courage to follow God into new territories—He has a plan.

"For I know the plans I have for you," declares the Lord, "plans to prosper you and not to harm you, plans to give you hope and a future.
Jeremiah 29:11 NIV

Thoughts

If you are working, what is your exit strategy? If not, what are your post retirement activities?

Fruitful

Trying to lead an interesting life, a fruitful life, is a big challenge.
John Patrick Shanley

Not only am I working in my career as a nurse at the writing of this book; but I am also moving further into my purpose of speaking and writing. All while helping to care for my 87-year-old mother who lives with me. At age 62 I published my first book and can feel many others competing to be released from my spiritual womb. It is a challenge to continue to write with my career and caregiver role. Though I go through seasons, God has empowered me to escape permanent stagnation. Satan is relentless with planting seeds of doubt about our ability to be fruitful during our seasoned years. God is faithful to fill us with new vision, new hope and purpose.

Then we wrestle diabolical doubt that our years will extend long enough to complete the vision that God has embedded within us. Then a flood of regret for not engaging in our Father's business—*sooner*. There are voices advising to forget about marriage because it will never happen. They can leave you feeling unworthy of a life partner and make you believe that you that you deserve to be alone. Satan warns that embracing hopes of a fulfilling relationship will surely end in disappointment. Does any of this sound familiar? If so, you are not alone. I constantly push past such rantings because I don't want to face the biggest regret of all.

The biggest regret of all—is ending your life without knowing what God **would** have accomplished through us had we only had the courage to **trust** Him. My goal is to publish at least 100 books—would love to do more! God has given me a word of encouragement for myself and His seasoned people. I would love to connect with someone along the way. If not be assured that I will be about my Father's Business! I will trust God with the details of my life and focus on bearing fruit that glorifies Him.

They shall still bring forth fruit in old age, they shall be fat and flourishing.
Psalms 92:14 KJV

Thoughts

Write about what you would like to accomplish in this season of life.

Balance

Everything in life has to have balance.
Donna Karan

There was a time that there were few enriching Christian events to attend in my small city. It's a new world! Our Sunday morning radio gospel show fills several segments to announce them all. Often several events occur the same day at the same time making it difficult to choose. There are those that try to make every event humanly possible to support ***everything***—and ***everybody.***

I'm learning to be led by the Holy Spirit when it comes to events. Changes occur during our seasoned years. Health issues, inherited responsibilities of caring for grandchildren or even our parents can lock our schedules. When God leads to attend an event, don't allow any of these things to restrict you. Find a way! But if dragging yourself from place to place is to others—think about it!

Some compromise their health, finances and even lose their lives by prioritizing events above their well-being. A person verbalized exhaustion from going to weeklong meetings. She was determined to attend the close out finale. The symptoms she ignored increased and she drove herself to the hospital *after* leaving the meeting and died in the emergency room.

Those with titles and leadership positions may feel obligated to make appearances—especially if it is sponsored by their church. This level of commitment is commendable. As a medical professional, I cringe when events are attended to the extent that people ignore their health.

There are conferences, appreciations, anniversaries and fundraisers ever among us. Without question attend when summoned by the Holy Spirit. Don't forfeit your health and life balance trying to attend ***everything.*** Pray—ask God to lead you in this area and every area of life- ***He will.***

Cause me to know the way wherein I should walk; for I lift up my soul unto thee.
Psalms 143:8 KJV

Thoughts

What keeps you from experiencing a sense of balance in your life?

Struggling

The triumph can't be had without the struggle.
Wilma Rudolph

My grandson is five at the writing of this book. He is preoccupied with the animal kingdom. Whether insects, jungle wildlife or creatures living in the oceans and seas he stares mesmerized for hours. He demands to watch such shows when he visits, I usually give in. If the animals are fighting—great! If eating each other—even better! Yielding to his desire, I have started to look forward to watching these shows with him. It's made me keenly aware of this one thing. *Everything* alive is struggling to survive.

When single we are acutely aware of the battles related to our journey and may minimize marital struggles. Those married are locked into the realities of couple skirmishes and may not be mindful of the combats engaged when living single. Whether married or single--Life is a struggle.

Committing your life to Jesus doesn't end struggles, it invites Him to join you amidst life's adversities. Whether waiting on God for a spouse, fighting for your marriage or engaged in the day to day battles of life—you are not in the fight alone. God knew that especially for his seasoned children that years of struggle would be challenging and tempt many to give up-don't! It is *always* too early to give up on God!

Now thanks be unto God, which always causeth us to triumph in Christ...
2 Corinthians 2:14 KJV

Thoughts

Can you identify some benefits you have you received from your life's struggles?

Respect

Most good relationships are built on mutual trust and respect.
Mona Sutphen

A friend was ambivalent about choosing a life partner. She was pursued by a man that had given her an engagement ring. There was also a man that she dated in high school who suddenly resurfaced leaving her ambivalent. "Do you respect him?" I asked when questioning her about the first person.

"I have more in common with Ryan and I respect him a lot more than John." (Fictitious names).

"Respect is important," I said, "You can fake liking a movie, you can fake enjoying certain foods, you can even fake an orgasm, but you cannot fake respect. A man will sense whether or not you respect him." We laughed while acknowledging that this is likely true.

I witnessed a senior couple who after 44 years of marriage they were contemplating divorce." She doesn't respect me." The husband concluded. His face was etched with lines of weariness. He had endured the castrating tongue of a bickering wife for years. It was a miracle that he managed to hang on so long. Living single for years can become wearisome.

Satan can convince you to settle for someone you know is incompatible just to escape loneliness. Be careful. Instead of an escape; you may find that you have imprisoned yourself to a lifetime sentence of remorse. Love, intimacy and holy matrimony will not thrive in a relationship where there is no respect. He will know. She will know. Women may face constant battle to withhold your tongue criticizing, condemning and verbally castrating his sense of manhood. Men may become butchers and shred a woman's self-worth—without speaking one word. Beware!

Show proper respect to everyone, love the family of belivers, fear God,
honor the emperor.
I Peter 2:17 NIV

Thoughts

Is it possible to rebuild a foundation of respect once you have lost respect for someone?

Marriage

There is no more lovely, friendly and charming relationship, communion or company than a good marriage.
Martin Luther

While anticipating a wonderful service, the raspy voice of the guest minister filtered the sanctuary. "God is healing marriages right now." A prolonged silenced lingered as the Holy Spirit ministered to our hearts individually.

"Not marriages, God, *not today!*" This statement was aimed toward the "*do-not-pertain-to-me basket.*" I struggled not to grab my stuff and exit. Was not in the mood for another service that would edify couples while leaving me and other singles to depart *unfulfilled.* Marriages are priorities for satanic attacks and I pray for them often. Yet I feel that singles also need specific ministry through local churches—even on Sunday sometimes. "Today, I need a word from You- for *M E!*"

"Thine Maker is thy husband." These words interrupted my mental protest. My relationship with my *husband- (God)* unfolded in the light of this scripture found in Isaiah 54:5. Lack of intimacy, too busy for quality time, limited trust and more were highlighted. The very ingredients necessary for a thriving marriage were deficient in my spiritual journey. My commitment level was not worthy to present to a mortal and certainly not befitting the King of Kings.

I am healthier spiritually when I attend to my relationship with God with the same dedication required to sustain a marriage. "God, forgive my despondency in *our* relationship, and please heal my marriage to You." I left the service enlightened, fulfilled with renewed motivation to build a more intimate union—with my Lord.

I will even betroth thee unto me in faithfulness: and thou shalt know the LORD.
Hosea 2:20 KJV

Thoughts

Do you feel that the spiritual needs of single Christians are under met by most local churches?

Me!

Nothing is cooler and more attractive than a big comeback, and that'll be me.
Steve Adler

It is the holiday weekend. I took Friday off so I could have five days off work to do *whatever*. What have I done so far? I hosted one of the longest and potentially destructive *pity parties* that I have held in a long time. It was quite pathetic. Why? Because it was all about *ME-ME-ME-EEE!!!* I had withdrawn so far inward that I feared that I would get lost and never find my way out. It felt like someone had ripped my heart out and left a throbbing vacuum. Satan loved every minute of it!

God prodded me throughout the day. ***Pray! Sing! Dance! Read scriptures! Do something! Do anything!*** I sunk further inside myself. I was scheduled to minister at the mission with a friend. I was excited at first—then I thought "How will God possibly pull even one encouraging word out of my mouth?" I felt numb.

It is not unusual for satan to crash through our emotional doors right before a ministry assignment. My friend and I ministered and prayed with women desperate for answers and facing serious challenges. Encouraging them snapped things back into perspective. Satan loves to entrap us with emotional blues, blinded to the great need in the world's field for ministry.

That day I started the process to speak monthly at the mission. It was a wonderful experience. God trusted me to speak life to His broken treasures. Satan's plan is to keep our focus inward while amplifying reasons to feel miserable. Maybe he torments you about how long you have been single? Perhaps his mocking leaves you feeling like no one cares. Or you may feel like you are *always* giving and *never* receiving. Whatever intent— it's a distraction. This journey, this life is not all about *ME* or *YOU*. Whatever season of life you have entered, whatever your situation, there is a place in the field for you. Allow God to use you—YES YOU...

The harvest truly is plentiful, but the laborers are few.
Luke 10:2 NIV

Thoughts

Make a list of things, activities and people that make you feel better to refer to when feeling down.

Why?

There are two great days in a person's life- the day we are born and the day we discover why.
William Barclay

"Why am I here?" This question emerges early in life and perplex many until their last breath. Yet it is no great mystery. God's purpose and plan for our lives was designed before our arrival into the physical world. It takes intimacy with our Creator to answer the whys? Yet we find ourselves amidst our seasoned years yet questioning the reason for our existence. We find clarity when we listen, focus and refuse distractions.

Ever notice that when moving towards purpose something or someone suddenly emerges. For singles it is often an unfortunate relationship. Satan use our natural inclinations as distractions to abort God's plans for us. This tactic to lead God's people astray has proven successful from the very beginning. Satan lured Eve into disobedience and then she became his instrument to distract Adam from his God-given assignment.

Eagerness to abandon the single journey can divert singles off the path that God has set before them. I have succumbed to such distractions over the years. It took years to rediscover God's path of purpose, plans and intent for my life. Many are destroyed before getting back. I am eternally grateful for God's grace. The writing ministry entrusted unto me was delayed for years.

Delayed by years of distractions and unhealthy relationships, I finally authored my first book at age sixty-two. I have learned to make the Father's business primary; relationships and everything else in my life are secondary to my purpose.

Stay on the path of purpose and trust God for genuine relationships that will not lead you off the path of His purpose; but those rich in mutual benefits able to compliment and support while bringing glory to His name.

Whether you turn to the right or to the left, your ears will hear a voice behind you saying, "This is the way; walk in it"
Isaiah 30:21 NIV

Thoughts

What forms of distractions have challenged you when on the path to purpose?

Swords

"Sometimes I lie awake at night, and ask, 'Where have I gone wrong?' Then a voice says to me, 'This is going to take more than one night.'"
Charles M. Schulz

"I am so stupid! I am not as intelligent as some people, I can't do anything right..." Initially, I didn't understand why this Christian woman was self-critical. Her constant verbal assaults against herself pierced me; I cannot imagine what they did to her. After hearing her story of years of verbal and emotional abuse by her deceased mother I got it. Her words merely echoed the sentiments embedded in her since childhood.

Negative words planted in her subconscious by her mother continued to speak, emotionally cripple and shred her self-worth from the grave. Voices in our heads have many origins. They come from parents, siblings, teachers, employers, friends and even ourselves. Satan is the originator of these destructive lies.

Such voices in are the very reason that it takes years to unveil the identity we have in Christ. Many never do. Our ongoing growth and development as singles and as human beings is dependent on how we respond to the conflicting inner voices we all experience. Some voices come to take you over and others to take you under. If the silent thoughts in your head are not victorious, overcoming thoughts, they are not from your Father, God.

Get rid of them- by meditating on God's word. Like swords words can pierce your spirit and causing it to leak all that is vital to your esteem. Defeat them! Just like satan uses words to harm, you can learn to use your words for self-healing. The Holy Spirit will teach you—Just ask! Begin today using the sword in your mouth—God's word.

Gracious words are a honeycomb, sweet to the soul and healing to the bones.
Proverbs 16:24 NIV

Thoughts

Have you been able to overcome the impact of negative words spoken over you in the past?

_____
_____
_____
_____
_____
_____
_____
_____
_____
_____
_____
_____
_____
_____
_____
_____
_____
_____
_____
_____
_____
_____

Vows

"Vows are powerful things." He said. "They set things in motion."
John C. Wright

A vow is "to make a determined decision or promise to do something," according to Cambridge Dictionary Online. A vow is used to describe the sacred words exchanged during a marriage ceremony. When receiving vows from others we want to believe they will honor their words by fulfilling the spoken commitment. But did you know that you can make a vow to yourself and that the power of those vows can control your life? Here is one example.

After crying for three days following the final separation from my husband; "I will never cry again!" I wiped my eyes and vowed on the third day. Normally a sensitive person who cried at the thought of a sad movie, my heart turned to stone on that day. It was ten years before I could conjure up a tear. Our words are powerful! We tend to live clueless of what we have activated with them.

Spoken words have no respect to whether they were used to be funny, in anger or absent mindedly...they have assignments to create what was said. During the course of our lives we say a lot of things that *seemingly* have no real impact on us—everyday! Take an inventory of what you have been speaking and compare them to the limitations in your life...your findings may surprise you.

You are snared by the words of your mouth.
Proverbs 6:2 NKJV

Thoughts

Identify anything manifested in your life birthed by your own words spoken in anger and pain?

Nevertheless

Thoughts

Are you standing at a fork in the road struggling to choose between your desires and God's will?

Beauty

The perception of beauty is a moral test.
Henry David Thoreau

"Do you think I'm pretty?" A middle-aged woman asked seeking a sincere response. Though she was beautiful inside and out; this attractive woman always felt unworthy and unappealing. She never sees anything positive in her photographs though they are remarkable.

"It doesn't matter what I think. Only what you think."

"Yes, it does!" she insisted.

I explained how many undergo the discomfort of plastic surgery to acquire what they perceive as physical beauty. Some experience amazing results only to continue to despise the person peering back through the mirror. After the financial investment and surgical distress, they are yet dissatisfied with the outcome. Many are permanently marred by repeated surgeries. It is said that "beauty is in the eye of the beholder."

It is vital that our beauty is seen through our own eyes by standards we define for ourselves. If not nothing anyone says will ever be convincing. The internet has photos of stars they deemed had aged poorly. Some of them had damaged their appearance with excessive tanning and repeated surgeries. Others had the appearance of the normal aging process and was pronounced to have "aged poorly." What pressure! The pursuit of eternal youth is a satanic strategy to cause us to align ourselves with thoughts and visions of insufficiency. Such images are implanted in our minds and bears fruit of dissatisfaction and self-rejection.

God's definition of beauty is not in sync with the world's. Ask God, "Do you think I'm pretty?" Or "handsome" if you are a guy. Regardless of your age or the impact of the aging process, the love and adoration of His response will overwhelm you!

Yet God has made everything beautiful for its own time.
Ecclesiastes 3:11 NLT

Thoughts

With mirror look into your eyes and speak words to affirm your inner and outer beauty. What did you feel? Write about it. Do this for 7 days.

Victorious

Victorious living does not mean freedom from temptation,
Nor does it mean freedom from mistakes.
E. Stanley Jones

"We will be having our first single's meeting this Saturday!" Our *married* pastor announced filled with enthusiasm. A few scattered applauses rose from the singles in the audience. "What's the matter with the single's, they don't sound very excited! We will be having our first single's meeting this Saturday!" He repeated and received pretty much the same stagnant response.

I don't know what was going through everyone else's mind- but I was dreading *another* class admonishing singles to abstain from fornication—as if this is the *only* real struggle we face. Especially when it is taught by a *lovey-dovey* couple and they graciously excuse themselves after teaching to pursue the undefiled marriage bed.

Abstinence is a major issue for singles. *We get this!* Yet there is so **much more** to living a victorious single Christian life. I am by no means advocating not attending classes presented by our *lovey-dovey married* pastors. I have received much strength and encouragement from couples ministering to singles. Some are really gifted in doing this without coming across as judgmental or condescending or clueless.

Yet, no one can encourage a single Christian, like another single Christian. One that is transparent while sharing the uncompromised word of God and seasoned with empathy, love, compassion and grace. There is a bond in knowing- we are in this—*together.* Let's encourage each other...

Now thanks be unto God, which always causeth us to triumph in Christ, and maketh manifest the savour of his knowledge by us in every place.
2 Corinthians 2:14 KJV

Thoughts

Do you attend single ministry functions? Why or Why not?

Counselor

I am surrounded by counselors. My sister is a counselor. My daughter is training to be a counselor. A lot of my friends are counselors.
Sue Townsend

"Maybe you should see a counselor," I suggested to a friend struggling with painful issues from her past. I can't afford it was among the responses I heard.

I am talking about the "Wonderful Counselor." She knew I was referring to Our Lord and Savior. We both laughed. Yet I was serious and shared with her how the Lord serves as my Counselor.

I worked mental health for over 20 years. I have seen some positive and negatives result in therapy. When faced with difficulties, often everyone in our lives will seek to counsel. The key is connecting with the right person.

There are times when I am in urgent need of a counselor. Though Counselors are effective they have limitations. They are limited by time, at the end of the hour you stuff your unresolved issues back inside and wait for the next appointment. They are limited by knowledge and experience and may not be able to facilitate you moving forward in certain areas.

Jesus is known as a "Wonderful Counselor," and I utilize Him as my full-time counselor. He is able and willing to counsel me ***anytime*** and ***anywhere*** about ***anything***. There are no limitations on how many times I can consult with him in a single day. He is a master at getting to the root of my issues and walking me through the pain. I am not dissing the profession of therapy.

I advocate counseling for issues that are too weighty to bear alone. If your journey results in you seeing a counselor, it's okay. Do what you need to heal! Just know that you have *The* Counselor available 24/7. Jesus is never distracted, shocked or overwhelmed by your dilemmas. He has answers to all the perplexing situations faced in this life. Just talk to Him.

And He will be called Wonderful Counselor...
Isaiah 9:6 KJV

Thoughts

Do you have someone to talk to about overwhelming situations? How do you handle stress?

Rest

Rest is not idleness, and to lie sometimes on the grass under the trees on a summer's day, listening to the murmur of water, or watching the clouds float across the sky, is by no means a waste of time"
John Lubbock

I drug inside the house after a tiring workday and dropped my heavy load of bags, purse and books on the sofa. I sighed while trying to shift gears. The hours left to devote to writing were few, I was beat; but I wanted to stick to my routine. It is good to stay busy when single; but balance is needed. I often plunged into overload by making excessive demands on myself that leave me depleted

Mentally and physically drained I strolled towards the computer. "Be still." I paused while cueing into this familiar inner prompting. "Sit in My presence, enter into My rest," it persisted. I glanced at the computer and walked away deciding to sit on the sofa instead and *rest*—a rare treat for me! Probing through my shopping bags I retrieved a random cassette. During lunch I grabbed several at a thrift store for twenty-five cents each— figured I couldn't lose for that price. After snapping it into the player, I pushed the "play" button.

The words, *"Be st-ill, and kn--ow that I a-m God..."* with soft worship music perfumed the room with the restorative presence of God. Exhaustion pulsated inside me like an automobile with a persistent low fuel alarm warning that refueling could no longer be postponed. Tears wet my cheeks as I basked in God's comfort and love, grateful that He cares enough to say, "Stop, sit, *rest- with Me.* God *always* knows exactly what you need... ***Listen.***

He maketh me to lie down in green pastures: he leadeth me beside the still waters. He restoreth my soul: he leadeth me in the paths of righteousness for his name' sake.
Psalm 23:2,3 KJV

Thoughts

Have you discovered the power of stillness? Lift your concern before God, quiet yourself and listen. Write what you hear.

Encouragement

If we are going to bring out the best in people, we need to sow seeds of encouragement.
Joel Osteen

"When I saw this. I wanted you to have it." The shop owner handed me a book shaped like a music box. I love books had and purchased many from him over the years. Lately, I was merely trudging through the motions of the Christian life. Uncertainty of God's love—for me was aggravating! No one knew--but God.

"God, I know you love the world' but what about me?" This question ricochet in my head—I couldn't shake it.

"Thank you." I accepted his thoughtful gift, wound the key and waited. Once released, "Jesus Loves Me..." this soft tune perfumed the room. This song hydrated my spirit while reviving my peace ending my long spiritual drought. I was deeply touched after thanking him I left soaring! Each time I recall God's unique way of reassuring me of His—ever-present love— I rejoice!

Singles withstand tremendous warfare in every arena of life. The intensity rises as seasoned years pounce upon us sooner than anticipated. This can result in feeling alone with unanswered questions. Small gestures to others having unknown significance can make a monumental impact.

This incident empowers me each time it resurges in my memory. It motivates me to practice showing kindness. Encouraging words, meeting a simple need, or a gentle touch can lift a broken spirit. Like me, many appear content when they are warring internally. Your acts of kindness may determine whether someone continues or drop out of the race of life altogether.

Everyone need reassurance that they are not alone. We know that that the Holy Spirit is an Encourager and Wonderful Friend. That's important— meanwhile never underestimate the power of being encouraged—*by a human.*

And we urge you, brothers and sisters, warn those who are idle and disruptive, encourage the disheartened, help the weak and be patient with everyone
I Thessalonians 5:14 NIV

Thoughts

Write about a time God used someone to remind you that He loves you.

Peace

When you've seen beyond yourself, then you may find peace of mind is waiting there.
George Harrison

Whether police, fire or ambulance, if it was a siren I just knew they were headed to— *my* house. This is what happens when life is lived in crisis mode! Wayward teens and damaging relationships and constant struggle can cause every avenue to peace to become inaccessible. This describes my life some years ago.

When I stepped into my journey as a single woman, the peace greeting me was frightening. I kept waiting for chaos to smash in and instantly turn my world upside down. Satan has many devices aimed toward destroying your peace. He offers the opposite of what God promises. Instead of peace He infest your life with fear and worry and will render you powerless.

How many years of your life have you spent worrying about things—that *never* happened? The Holy Spirit is teaching me to use my mental faculties for activities other than worry. Like basking in the peace of God, visualizing a prosperous future and anticipating fulfilling my divinely orchestrated purpose.

The peace of God is *real.* There are yet times when it seems like everything is falling apart. Things are *rarely* as they seem. I retreat into that secret place with God only to discover that when it is all said and done— everything was falling into place. Guard your peace, rely on God, you *can* trust Him.

You will keep him in perfect peace whose mind is stayed on You, because he trusts in You.
Isaiah 26:3 NKJV

Thoughts

Would you say that you have experienced more, or less peace since your journey as a single person?

_____
_____
_____
_____
_____
_____
_____
_____
_____
_____
_____
_____
_____
_____
_____
_____
_____
_____
_____
_____
_____

Fireproof

"I survived because the fire inside me burned brighter than the fire around me."
Joshua Graham

I been through fires. At times I feared I would be consumed in my entirety! The three Hebrews were cast into a fiery furnace. It was described as seven times hotter than it ought to be. That spoke volumes to me of just how much satan hates us. Fire will destroy flesh and blood quickly and I imagined a fiery death is horrendous. Why make it hotter? Pure hatred.

Yes, sometimes fires of this life get much hotter than what seems humanly bearable. You may feel certain that you will not survive. As singles we come from an assortment of challenges that at the time may feel all consuming. Some lose loving spouses and don't believe they have the momentum to continue life alone. Some experiences painful divorces from marriages they thought would last forever.

Others barely escaped with their lives from brutal abuses of all sorts. The list of fires that we have survived is massive. We each have a story to tell. With God I have walked through blazes with courage and a smile. When the smoke cleared there was no evidence that I was ever engulfed by tormenting flames of tribulation. God loves us and even when life swallows us with fires—hotter than they ought to be—He is there.

When you walk through the fire, you will not be burned; the flames will not set you ablaze.
Isaiah 43:2 NIV

Thoughts

What are some positive outcomes that you can see in your life after coming out of a fiery trial?

_____
_____
_____
_____
_____
_____
_____
_____
_____
_____
_____
_____
_____
_____
_____
_____
_____
_____
_____
_____

Menopause

"Every woman's menopause experience is unique. That's where the confusion comes from. People experience symptoms at different times."
Pamela Boggs

"The woman said, "I've already been through menopause, one; day I paused and thought about all the men in my life."

"That's cute," I thought, until I discovered that this middle age woman was not kidding! Wish to God menopause was that simple! Depression, hot flashes, moodiness- if not informed about this rite of passage it can cause your whole world to collapse leaving you mystified.

Men may also experience menopausal symptoms right down to hot flashes. Our bodies enter new phases over the years. A friend introduced me to a natural remedy that coasted me through the onslaught of these menacing symptoms. Menopause is no joke; but rather a riddle. The answer is varies from person to person.

Women have been admitted to mental health units depressed, crying and unable to identify why? Some were treated with multiple medications attempting to restore emotional and physical balance. Many are discharged with marginal or no improvement.

Our bodies are mysterious! The amazing journey through the stages of life become less fearful and more wonderful as we pray for understanding to adapt and respond with wisdom to this physical transition common to most.

> I praise you because I am fearfully and wonderfully made; your works are wonderful, I know that full well.
> Psalm 119:14 NIV

Thoughts

About every seven years we enter a new season of life. What new skills and knowledge do you need to effectively master your current season?

Cake

"Mourning is the constant reawakening that things are now different."
Stephanie Ericsson

In her book "Let's Roll" Lisa Beamer shared a memory about her children. After celebrating the birthday of her deceased husband with her two small children she became tearful. "Why are you crying? The older son asked, she explained that she missed their father and was feeling sad." With the innocence that only a child can master he asked, "We can still have cake, can't we?" I found this to be simplistic, yet powerful!

I have talked to widows both men and women who experience the vacuum of a deceased spouse. The depth of their pain is palpable. They are launched into a season of involuntary solitude while shouldering finances and other responsibility that were once shared. God has great compassion for widows. To the extent that ministering to the needs of widows is the very definition of *"true religion."* If you are single and yet unclear of your purpose. Start here.

Pray and ask God for a widow or orphan to encourage *today*. He will be well pleased with your service to them during this extremely distressful season.

Whether widowed or experiencing the death of a significant relationship, there are yet sweet things in life to partake. Don't deny yourself to partake the sweeter things in life. Your mate would not wish that for you. It's okay…you can still eat cake.

Pure and genuine religion in the sight of God the Father means caring for orphans and widows in their distress and refusing to let the world corrupt you.
James 1:27 NIV

Thoughts

Are you allowing loss of any kind (death of a loved one, divorce, death of a dream, financial, spiritual) caused you to deny yourself the sweeter things of life?

_____
_____
_____
_____
_____
_____
_____
_____
_____
_____
_____
_____
_____
_____
_____
_____
_____
_____

Prayer

True prayer is neither a mere mental exercise nor a vocal performance. It is far deeper than that—it is spiritual transaction with the Creator of Heaven and Earth.
Charles Spurgeon

It was late, but I wanted to spend some intimate time with God before bed. I will pray after I finish my cup of tea. I felt God drawing me, "Come, bring your tea," I sensed in my spirit. I did. I shared a wonderful fellowship with my Heavenly Father, tea and all.

Another time I fell into bed and began to pour out my frustrations and stopped mid-sentence saying, "God, I don't have to explain because You already know."

"This is true" I sensed in my spirit. The Bible says God knows our thoughts even before we think them. Yet I sensed Him encouraging me, to pour out my heart to Him.

"Yes, I do, but I want you to talk to me." I find peace in the knowledge that God cares about the details of my life. There is nothing to minute to discuss with Him. There is no conversation too long for Him. No one in the world will ever love you so much that they never tire of your voice. That they love the sound of your voice so deeply that they never tire of it.

God knows exactly how we feel; but talk to Him anyway. There are areas of our heart that we have yet to surrender to Him. He stands at the door knocking and waiting to enter to converse with you about any issues pertaining to your life. No matter what kind of marital partner God blesses you with—no one will *ever* desire to talk to you as much as Him.

Behold I stand at the door and knock. If anyone hears My voice and opens the door, I will come in to him and dine with him, and he with Me.
Revelation 3:20 NIV

Thoughts

There is no greater gift that we can offer God than to <u>enjoy</u> spending time with Him? List some creative ways to fellowship with God.

Addictions

No one is immune from addiction, it afflicts people of all ages, races, classes and professions.
Patrick J. Kennedy

"Come with me tonight?" My friend often invited. Gambling slithered into my life disguised as an innocent kiddy game—*Bingo*. She magnified her winnings and gleamed while talking about the great time she has.

"I don't think so," graciously declining her invitation for the umpteenth time. Then—one day—no special reason, I said "*Yes*." This impulsive moment changed the course of my life. I regretted it for the next ten years. Gambling began consuming my life until I became imprisoned by this game of chance.

Addictions come in many forms. Common additions are drugs, food, tobacco, alcohol and gambling. There are endless things that can lead to unhealthy addictions shopping, exercising, tanning, plastic surgery, tattoos, video games, social media and yes there are even sexual addictions.

There are many reasons that people become ensnared by addictions. Depression, loneliness and seeking escape from a dissatisfying lifestyle are among them. It can take ten years before the full impact of addictions unveil and burst through the fortified walls of denial. By this time many are in too deep.

Addictions can result in the loss of family, jobs, finances and even lives. Addictions penetrates through age, financial, racial, political or religious barriers. You may find that you have more than one addiction. Whatever your addiction, whatever your struggle; Jesus is the answer. You will never get in too deep that His grace cannot reach and restore your shattered life.

It is of the Lord's mercies that we are not consumed, because His compassions fail not.
They are new every morning: great is thy faithfulness.
Lamentations 3:22, 23 KJV

Thoughts

Addictions take many forms. Nicotine, drugs, food, sex, gambling. Write a prayer for any addictions you desire God to deliver you or someone else from.

Clarity

My Pastor once said, "make up your mind what you want, then walk away from everything else... makes sense..."

Thoughts

Often the focus is on what we do not want. Make a list of qualities you DESIRE in a marital partner.

_____
_____
_____
_____
_____
_____
_____
_____
_____
_____
_____
_____
_____
_____
_____
_____
_____
_____
_____
_____

Treasures

"I'm an ocean, because I'm really deep. If you search deep enough you can find rare exotic treasures."
Christina Aguilera

In the Bible there are narratives given about many of the kings. I found a common theme that pertains to war. The treasure of the defeated king was confiscated, and the king paraded with his robe cut off exposing his buttocks. Sometimes half of the beard was shaved for further humiliation. This was also done to David's men who were captured in 2 Samuel 10:4.

We are kings and priest This paints a picture of how satan wants to strip you of every precious thing God has placed inside. Your gifts, talents and dreams are treasures that God instilled in you before birth. Once these are stolen satan he wants your dignity. His ultimate goal is to confiscate your faith which is your most precious treasure. It is important that we war to protect our faith. This is the treasure that satan wishes to apprehend. He knows that without it you will not be effective in receiving from God.

It is the same way with satan when he launches attacks against us if we allow him victory he does not leave empty handed. He wants to take away something. Even if he chisels away at your self-worth and carries it away in bits and pieces. Until one day you arise, and you don't feel worthy to look another person in the eyes.

What about your faith... It is certainly the greatest treasure we possess, for without it is impossible to please God. In fact, God values our faith as much more precious than pure gold.

Proceed with caution and let nothing or no one cause you to abruptly fling aside your faith! It is the most precious treasure that you will ever possess.

The trial of your faith, being much more precious than of gold that perished, though it be tried with fire, might be found unto the praise and honor and glory at the appearing of Jesus Christ.
I Peter 1:7 KJV

Thoughts

Write about treasures satan has stolen from you. How are you using your FAITH to reclaim them?

Incredible

The journey has been incredible from its beginning.
Sidney Poitier

My sister relocated to California after getting married years ago. She decided to stay following her divorce. Lisa graduated from college and fulfilled her dream of teaching while supporting four children. She shared the following incident.

"I was working full time and going to school while juggling bills. Lord, I just need fifty or sixty more dollars to meet expenses this month. I noticed something on the side of the road while driving. It looked like money trapped in a bush—I wasn't sure.

I figured that if it was money that someone would pick it up before I turned around."

"Go back." This prompting rose inside—I did.
"I pulled up to the side of the road where the green image first grabbed my attention. It was a one-hundred-dollar bill standing upright against a bush—I was shocked! *Too good to be true,* was my first thought. "Can't be real!" To prove it, I drove to the bank. "Would you check to see if this is real?" I explained that I found it.

"It's real and since you have no way of contacting the owner I guess it is yours!" My sister expressed sincere gratitude for this demonstration of God's love and provision. This is just one of many incredible stories she shares reporting the Faithfulness of God in her life. Single parents don't always have the luxury of a second income to help with expenses. Others don't always see the despair created by lack of finances- *God does.*

The one who calls you is faithful, and he will do it.
I Thessalonians 5:24 NIV

Thoughts

Have you experienced incredible answers to prayer? Write about one.

Straight

In the middle of the journey of our life I came to myself
Within a dark wood where the straight way was lost.
Dante Alighieri

Life without God proved futile. Initially, my boyfriend abused alcohol and marijuana. When he launched into other drugs; life became unbearable. Like a fly in a jar with the lid screwed *tight-* I felt trapped. We moved to Joy Road on Sweetest Day. Could this be an omen that the traumatic course of our lives was changing for the *better?* I deluded myself, while clinging desperately to the *"happily-ever-after"* ending tucked safely in my mind. It never manifested.

While nearing the end of our ten-year history, I sunk deeper into gambling behaviors to escape the pain of my day to day existence. Though I missed it, I was not attending church during these years. I wanted to organize my life better- *first.* Each effort to restore order resulted in greater chaos. At the culmination of this relationship I felt like just one more tragedy would destroy me. My strength was consumed with daily efforts to merely survive.

One night my heart cried out the words of the scripture written below to the Living God. When I awakened throughout the night I heard my inner spirit pleading these very words. I knew something detrimental was on the brink if change did not come. In answer to the petition of my heart, the next day was to be our *final* separation. God began the reorganization of my upside-down world. He shed light into the darkness, bought down the mountains, exalted the valleys, and yes, He even made the crooked places straight. I love Him!

"I will go before thee, and make the crooked places straight..."
Isaiah 45:2 KJV

Thoughts

Are you staying in a painful relationship now or in the past, hoping something magical will happen?

_____
_____
_____
_____
_____
_____
_____
_____
_____
_____
_____
_____
_____
_____
_____
_____
_____
_____
_____

Rebound

**To spring or bounce back after hitting or colliding with something.
To recover, as from depression or disappointment.
American Heritage Dictionary**

Ever felt full of passion and purpose? Then a situation comes and knock the wind out of you leaving you flat on my back— metaphorically. The problem is not being floored; but taking *so-ooo* long to bounce back between these situations.

Rebound means to "bounce back after hitting a hard surface, to return to a better level or position, to spring back, as from a sudden impact." (Macmillan online dictionary). Time moves forward, whether we choose to- or not. As we get older the ability to rebound and pick up where you left off and quickly readjust becomes even more critical.

Failed relationships happen, they are painful; but don't carry that burden forever! Some singles get up and rush right back into the same or another doomed connection and acquire an accumulation of pain. One pastor gave this example. "If you were crossing the street and fell, would you just sit there?"

Those passing by would question, "Why are you *just* sitting there?" Day after day, year after year many sit in the very place that they fell into rejection, abuse, unfaithfulness or other encounters that can dismantle a relationship and leave you floored. Sitting and mentally replaying the fall is not the answer. Let go! Get up! Move on! God has more for you. In the words of Jesus, *"Take up thy bed and walk!"*

**The Lord upholdeth all that fall and rasiseth up all those that be bowed down.
Psalm 145:14 KJV**

Thoughts

Is there a current situation that you need to ask God to help you rebound?

Disabilities

"Disability is a matter of perception. If you can do just one thing well,
you're needed by someone."
Martina Navratilova

It is easy for onlookers to make soothing statements about disabilities like the one above. The validity of such words is evident in the lives of many who accomplish amazing feats despite physical challenges. Physical challenges of any sort can result in life being a tedious journey—for some it is even more tedious. Some people have given up hope of having a successful relationship. I had a conversation with a man who was paralyzed.

"Who is looking for somebody in a wheelchair to marry!" He's erected years of frustrations from coping with his long-term disability.

"Guess what I saw on TV last week!" I shared this story. The parents allowed their five-year old daughter to have her legs amputated at the hips rather than have her bound to a wheelchair. They promoted independence and self-confidence. As an adult she not only drove but also learned to repair cars.

She used her hands to get around and didn't mind going places alone. She shared how she met her husband while dining *alone* in a restaurant. A tall, handsome man connected with her and they were an adorable couple." I don't know how this story impacted him. I hope it shed even a little encouragement.

It is not only physical disabilities that produce thoughts and fears of, *"What if... I never meet anyone..."* These are thoughts that satan plants in the heart and minds of every single desiring a healthy marriage. Watching the couple on TV made me think of the faithfulness of God.

Over the years I have crossed paths with people with both mental and physical disabilities that found love and shared a meaningful relationship with someone. Whether our disabilities are lodged in our bodies or minds—Don't allow disabilities to blind you to life's possibilities.

For nothing is impossible with God.
Luke 1:37 NLT

Thoughts

Do you fear that your journey as a single is permanent because of a perceived disability? Write about it. Include struggles with weight problems.

Kisses

This smooth skinned, slimy creature that lurks in murky waters has been the focus of many fairy tales.

I read many fairy tales as a child. One thing that amazed me was the power of a kiss. A kiss awakened sleeping beauty, turned frogs into handsome princes, horrid witches instantly became fair maidens and let's not forget about the transformed beast.

We often grow up with unrealistic expectations ingrained in our subconscious and too often overestimate the power of a kiss. Your kiss is not powerful enough to break cycles of physical, emotional or sexual abuse. Kisses do not magically create faithfulness in a cheating woman or man. A kiss will not transform a person with a dark heart into a person of light and beauty.

Whether male or female our kisses are not powerful enough to bring spells of dysfunctional behaviors. The intoxicating tingling of the flesh produced by kissing has only one hidden power—the power of seduction. Whether in fairy tales or real life sometimes we learn the hard way- that a frog is just a slimy creature and a witch is only good for casting spells.

Your kiss will not break the power of addiction, stop physical, emotional or sexual abusive behaviors or make someone who doesn't really love you treat you with respect. If this is you, pray for the strength to walk away and move on. No matter how long you have been spellbound by his or her kisses...God can break the spell and set you free!

> He reached down from the heavens and rescued me.
> Psalm 18:16 NLT

Thoughts

Do you think that we can deceive ourselves into believing that passionate acts of affection will cause another to change?

Legitimate

Sex is wonderful, but I want you to know that sex must be held in proper perspective—that is, within a marital relationship where male and female have first committed themselves to one another spiritually, emotionally, and intellectually.
Greg Speck

"Just get married!" This simplistic solution is often tossed to new Christians in live-in arrangements soon after receiving salvation. I cringe—whenever I hear this. Marrying the *right* person is a *far* greater issue than legitimizing sexual interactions.

"Marry me?" I heard this often during the course of the ten years we lived together. Sure—I *was* miserable, but desires to please God and resume right standing with Him were overpowering. Constant wrestling with guilt and condemnation would finally cease—I reasoned. I seriously considered marriage. Through God's grace— I never did! I was spared marriage to an incompatible person—a second time.

In these situations, marriage is *not* the *right* answer for *everyone*. God's plan may be to rescue an individual out of a relationship that He knows will only yield disappointment and heartbreak. If this describes your situation—it is your decision to have the courage to walk away.

There is no *real* gain in legitimized sex— with the *wrong* person. The greatest way to honor the covenant of marriage... is to enter it with the right motives, right priorities and the right person. Legitimate sex—is one consideration—but should not be the *only* one when converting a live-in situation into a marriage.

Marriage should be honored by all, and the marriage bed kept pure, for God will judge the adulterer and all the sexually immoral.
Hebrews 13:4 KJV

Thoughts

Write a prayer for those conflicted in live in relationships that God will give them clear directions.

Praise

The sweetest of all sounds is praise.
Xenophon

I'm guilty of dashing back and forth to work with money to pay bills while missing the deadlines. Unlike couples, many singles do not have someone working alongside them maintain balance in their world. While working a horribly stressful job. I would take praise breaks throughout the day. (I still do!) God sustained me as I continued to focus on Him. I praised and thanked Him throughout the day.

During this season I discovered that my water bill was past due. I made time to go to the office the following day. When I offered payment, the clerk was explaining when my water would be turned back on. "My water is not off," I explained. The clerk examined the records closer. Then reported that they sent someone to shut my water off—but the attempt was unsuccessful. I never heard of such a thing!

This blessed me and continues to be a precious memory of the Faithfulness of God. God is mindful of us and our needs—even when we forget. Praise is a powerful! When we keep our focus on God even amidst stressful situations, He has unique ways of caring for us. Don't allow satan to sow seeds of frustration in your heart. Though single you are never alone.

Though entering seasoned years—God will not forsake us. He is working behind the scenes on your behalf—*even now.* Keep praising Him!

Evening, and morning, and at noon, will I pray, and cry aloud: and
He shall hear my voice.
Psalm 55:17 KJV

Thoughts

Schedule three times a day when you will intentionally turn your mind and heart towards God and praise Him for His goodness.

Interruptions

*"Don't allow others to interrupt you in the vision. Whatever it
Cost it must be obtained. Nothing in life is free.
Lester Surmall*

Interruptions can come in many forms. They can be disguised with critical labels that could have been easily delegated or handled at a more feasible time. Interruptions can come from within or without. The problem with interruptions is that they can deter you from the path of God's vision and purpose.

When snatched off your set course from either an inner or outer interruption, delays can be days, weeks, months or even years before the discipline to refocus returns. Sometimes the path is never trodden again because of the inability to regain lost drive, motivation or purpose.

My most deadly interruptions are those attacking me from within. Writing is subject to constant interruptions and books can be delayed for years. Or even worse never completed at all. Social media is another *major* source of interruptions. I mostly write on my laptop and sometimes I plan to take a quick peek at Facebook, YouTube or some other site- big mistake! Sometimes it is hours before I emerge and often fail to do what I originally intended.

The ability to focus and effectively juggle interruptions will determine the progress we make toward achieving our goals. I have perfected the art of saying *"No"* to others when necessary, but until I can say "no" to the interruptions arising from inside— my ability to witness the fruit of my labor will be hindered.

*Therefore my beloved brethren, be ye stedfast, unmoveable, always abounding in the work of the Lord, forasmuch as ye know that your labour is not in vain in the Lord.
I Corinthian 15:58 KJV*

Thoughts

Has technology been a source of increased interruptions in your life? If so, how can you decrease it?

Thoughts

When is the last time that you did something REALLY exciting? Plan a new venture!

Feelings

*The biggest disease this day and age is that
of people feeling unloved.*
Princess Diana

I once belonged to a church that concluded services with everyone praying around the altar. One night everyone seemed to receive a special touch from God...*except me*. My heart ached while *feeling* unloved and forsaken by God.

Dragging myself toward the door I fought back tears of rejection. Then I heard a tune I sang as a child. *"No never alone, no never alone, I promise never to leave you, never to leave you alone."* I turned wondering if anyone else heard the melody. Then I realized this soothing melody originated in my heart and cancelled my *feelings* of alienation.

Living alone over the years may cause toxic emotions to seek entry into your heart. News of wedding, engagements and anniversaries circulate, and it *feels* like everyone's getting married—except you. Of course, satan reminds you that "you are not getting any younger. This can result in feelings of polluted by feelings of loneliness, alienation, insecurity and more.

Such FEELINGS can cause pain and may result in thoughts like, "there must be something wrong with me! What if I am single forever!" At times you may feel like the ONLY single person left on the planet! FEELINGS are deceitful, this is why God instructs us to live by faith and not FEELINGS.

Jesus promised to never leave us alone is faithful to keep this commitment. Even when you feel alone – He's there. Jesus will comfort, strengthen and sustain you through each season of life. As I grow and develop in the knowledge of Him my ability to stand on His promises even when I *feel* alone is increasing. *lings.* My relationship with God extends far beyond mere *feelings*. Whether or not I *feel* like it— I *know* God is *ALWAYS* with me!

"...Lo, I am with you always, even unto
the end of the world." Amen.
Matthew 28:20 KJV

Thoughts

Many singles feel "alone" at times. How do you handle these feelings?

Elephants

People are so difficult give me an elephant any day.
Mark Shand

I read a story in which the female character was engaged to be married and she dreamt that her fiancé was trying to find a house big enough for her *elephant.* Interesting. But when you think about it, as perfect as we see ourselves (joke), we *all* have issues. Though the details escape me, this story found a space in my mind that it has claimed over the years.

Our irks and quirks may be barely noticeable to us; but for another— it may be an elephant! I watched a reality show where a couple was matched and had to determine if they were going to remain together. During meals the man smacked his lips which was an *elephant* to the woman. Though they had many other compatibilities this was *one* concern she will have to overcome if she decides to continue the relationship.

Living single for so many years, I imagine I have an entire herd! If you are romanticizing and fantasizing about happily-ever-after—plant your feet back on the ground and face the fact that we are *all* come with an *elephant* or two. Until we accept the fact that we are all imperfect—we are not ready for a healthy relationship.

Some things are just deal breakers right from the get-go; yet there will be imperfections in ourselves and others that will have to be accepted to enjoy moving forward—*together.*

Love never fails.
I Corinthian 13:8 NIV

Thoughts
What are YOUR elephants?

College

You must do things that you think you cannot.
Eleanor Roosevelt

When I first accepted Jesus into my heart, it was such a beautiful experience! I anticipated His return and felt like it could be any moment. I had dropped out of high school in the twelfth grade and did not have any aspirations for higher education. I was the 3rd oldest of eight children and no one had attended college—yet. Why bother—Jesus is coming *SOON!* I heard this preached time and time again and was looking for my Savior's return any day!

God helped me to get my head out of the clouds and refocused on my journey in this world. Allowing God to order my steps resulted in earning a college degree and a nursing career. All while anticipating the return of Christ.

Whether you are waiting on a life partner or the Savior of the world; don't put off going to college if this is the desire of your heart. You are not too old! I graduated with someone in their 80's. I am sixty-four and yet entertain the possibility of returning to school. Once earned that college degree is *yours.* Choose an educational path that will accentuate your God-given gifts and equip you for your divine purpose.

Uniting with the *right* life partner is just one facet of life—it's a *biggy!* But not *everything!* Don't let discouragement, disillusion or depression paralyze you during the single experience—keep moving forward with your education! Once you meet someone special you will be happy that this is crossed off your list. More time to invest and enjoy creating a healthy relationship.

The heart of the discerning acquires knowledge, for the ears of the wise seek it out.
Proverbs 18:15 NIV

Thoughts

Are you putting college, training or any higher learning goals on hold for any reason? Why?

Therefore

I think, therefore I am.
Rene Descartes.

There are times during this journey when you may punch the "override" button and disregard the caution the Holy Spirit. I am guilty! It is no coincidence that the same devil that coerce you into venturing into his territory will mock and taunt you once you are wrestling with guilt and shame. The book of Ephesians warns that our battle is against dark wicked spiritual forces. Satan has convinced many that a battle against spiritual influences is foolery and nonexistent.

As the wolf told Little Red Riding Hood, "the better to eat you my dear!" Not only to eat you, but to literally destroy every aspect of your live and the lives of those you hold dear. Over the years I have used the word *"therefore"* in the scripture below as a reminder of what I am standing *"there for."* I am standing to demonstrate to my children and children's children that God will redeem you. He forgives the sins of youth and continue to love, protect and provide for us all the days of our lives. I am standing because of the love God has shown me throughout my journey with Him—Even when I was not the most obedience.

I am stand *therefore* because I know that there is a divine purpose for my life and I will never know it in its totality unless I stand "there for" it. I am standing to prove to future generations that it is *always* a good decision to serve God.

Stand therefore...
Ephesians 6:14 KJV

Thoughts

What are you standing "THERE FOR?" Make a list and refer to it when you feel like giving up.

Pain

"I don't think we can get there without any pain."
Joe Nation

"Are you going to hurt me?" He questioned as we moved forward at warp speed with passions as hot as the boiling heat of volcanic lava. What kind of question was that? Who goes into a relationship with the intent of inflicting pain? Well, I am sure that those sorts exist; but I think that most venture in seeking a refuge from loneliness desiring to abide in a sanctuary of love. Yet despite our best efforts—we hurt each other.

If asked this question from a potential partner again—I would answer honestly and without hesitation. "Yes, I'm going to hurt you—but not intentionally." What two people even with the best of relationship skills have *not* caused pain? Intentional or not, it happens. A better question is, "Are you going to forgive me?" Forgiveness is the antidote; when used properly it prevents an accumulation of pain.

A minister shared the response of Ruth Graham when asked if she ever considered divorce. "Divorce, no. Murder, yes." Humorous. Often people enter relationships dazzled by the effects of the hormonal changes that occur within the sexes once attraction occurs. While under this spell the thought of causing or receiving pain from each other seems highly unlikely.

I am certainly not referring to the pain of emotional, physical abuse, perpetually cheated on or blatant disrespect. Yet becoming one in a relationship is a beautiful, transformative process laced with pain and forgiveness. Being human affords us ample opportunities to practice dealing with both intentional and unintentional pain. Master this skill! Whether the relationship is from church, work, family or other, you will need it!

Be kind and compassionate to one another, forgiving each other,
just as in Christ God forgave you
Ephesians 4:32 NIV

Thoughts

What have you learned about dealing with pain in relationships of any sort?

_____
_____
_____
_____
_____
_____
_____
_____
_____
_____
_____
_____
_____
_____
_____
_____
_____
_____
_____
_____

Epiphany!

A moment when you suddenly realize or understand something important.
Macmillan Online Dictionary

"Tell me about yourself." Invitations for self-disclosures choked me. Words formed in my head and became trapped inside my mouth. Embarrassing! After all I *am* an adult! It's *always* been difficult to enjoy meaningful conversations with men. My past is laced with horrendous traumas that made me fear immediate rejection.

Epiphany! It occurred while reading Dr. John Gray's book, "Men are from Mars and Women are from Venus." He compared the healing qualities of love with receiving salvation. When a woman risk expressing past traumas and failures to her partner and His response is unconditional love and acceptance—she is healed. This also occurs if the man is vulnerable and received with love and acceptance

My mind flashed to my salvation. I repented for my sins and felt unbearable shame and remorse. Every sinful memory and failure presented to God was met without reservation with love. This revelation liberated and equipped me to find greater ease when talking with men. Whoever *God* sends to me or you will be able to cover us with love. We must be willing to do the same. Love is healing, restorative and transformational!

Most important of all, continue to show deep love for each other, for love makes up for many of your faults.
I Peter 4:8 TLB

Thoughts

In your seasoned years, would you say that it's more, or less difficult to talk with someone expressing an interest in you?

Birth

Gratitude to gratitude always gives birth.
Sophocles

There was a season when poetry flowed effortless from my spirit. I awoke from sleep writing. Carried a pen and paper—everywhere. I wanted to capture—everything! Many of the poems I've written to date came forth during this season of supernatural release. It was like a constant birthing and this caused me to become a little weary. God, I need a rest I requested in my stupidity!

He gave me a rest alright. It was years before I was inspired to write another poem! Perhaps it's offensive to ask God to hold back on creativity—He is after all, *The Creator.*

When your spirit is ready to give birth it's difficult not to engage in the writing process. All you can think about is release and pushing into the physical realm what has been resting in your spiritual womb. A pregnant woman would never ignore the pain and pressure that signifies it is time for delivery. No excuse would be acceptable! That child is coming forth!

How many projects die in our spiritual womb because we abort the process? Whether books, art, music, plays, conferences, workshops, trainings, businesses, ministries and so on. Years of creativity traded for barrenness, what a loss! It is God's will that we *ALL* give birth to something. Though not as free flowing as once experienced; I did tap into the ability to write poetry again. I am grateful.

What ever creative abilities God has given you; don't allow satan to belittle them in your mind by comparing them to others. We never know how God will use our creations for His divine purposes. Trust Him and when He says push—*PUSH!* It is time to give birth...

For we are God's masterpiece. He has created us anew in Christ Jesus so that we can do the good things He planned for us long ago.
Ephesians 2:10 NIV

Thoughts

Are there forms of creativity that you no longer tap into? If so, ask God to call them forth.

Offence

People seem to take as much offence as they possibly can these days—it's almost a new type of greed, a new kind of road rage.

We live in a world where Buddha, Allah or deities from any other faith are openly discussed without social repercussions. There is no hype when these graven images are openly displayed. But just say the name of JESUS. Our world has changed and today references to God or His Son are whispered—to avoid *offending* anyone. Darkness is certainly covering the earth. Satan's intent is to weaken Christianity at its very roots and to lessen its impact on delivering humanity from His evil clutches.

This is no accident. Over the years I have had opportunity to watch satan's seductive and well executed plans of deception. They were operating full force in my life until God rescued me. My life would have likely ended long ago or else stretched over years with one terrible outcome after another. My path of destruction was intercepted by God.

Jesus is the point of reference for *everything* good that pertains to me. Though some may find Him offensive, no way could I *ever* exclude Jesus from *any* aspect of my human experience. Satan has been longsuffering and strategic with achieving this goal.

And blessed is he, whoever shall not be offended in me.
Matthew 11:6 KJV

Thoughts

Have you encountered someone being offended by your faith? How did you feel?

Accommodation

Darkness cannot drive out darkness only light can do that.
Martin Luther King Jr.

Our physical eyes have an ability to gradually adjust to darkness. This is a very useful ability when you find yourself in a place where the lights are suddenly turned off. The world has become a very dark place. As time progresses; the darker it becomes. We are living in a time when a generation is being raised without the foundations of morality that were once considered norms.

Those who are on the path of singleness may find themselves losing their way in these times where the lines of obedience to God have been blurred by terms like *tolerance* and *politically correct*. The spiritual sight of many has adjusted to the gradual descent of darkness to the degree that the increasing darkness is barely noticeable.

Christians enter relationships where there are clear incompatibilities. The things that once topped the *"deal breaker"* list are now *"tolerable."* Abstinence is viewed as an aberration and a foolish practice by some. This has caused some singles to delude themselves into to believing that sex before marriage is acceptable. The bible foretold of gross darkness that would cover the earth. It is only one way to overcome darkness and that is to turn on the light. You are the candles that God use to illuminate the darkness. Own it, profess it—*SHINE!*

Arise and shine for your light has com, and the glory of the Lord has risen upon you.
Isaiah 60:1 NIV

Thoughts

Are there times when you know that you are choosing not to let your light shine?

WAR!

**Warfare has been waged
The thing that you will find
It's not fought with knives & guns
But right within your mind...**

Thoughts

What spiritual weapons do you use to overcome mental warfare?

"When we become Passionate About God's Purpose...

He Becomes Purposeful About Our Passions..."

About the Author

Jeri has confronted challenges common to singles who have been single long-term. Single, married, separated and divorce are paths that Jeri has known during her 25 years of living single. If your single journey has stretched much longer than you ever anticipated and headed towards double digits—This book was written for you. Seasoned years greet you with a host of new needs and challenges.

Perhaps your health is faltering, or you find yourself in a caregiver role that you didn't see coming. Maybe your heart has turned to stone from emotional pain and trust is no longer an option. These brief devotions are followed by a writing prompt to facilitate excavating buried emotions.

Jeri is passionate about encouraging God's seasoned people to get off the sidelines of life and get back in the race to fulfill their God-Given purpose. On Mondays at 2 PM EST Jeri does an inspiration Facebook live video proclaiming to others that they are "seasoned for this season! Regardless of age, failures or marital status—God yet has a purpose for our lives.

Jeri is a registered nurse with over 25 years' experience in the mental health field. She has ministered to men and women in jail, prison, halfway houses and shelters. Jeri has ministered at single's conferences and written and directed plays addressing issues related to singles. She is the author of Stepping Stones Reflections for Singles which was written during the earlier years of her single experience.

Jeri has also been published in 'Chicken Soup for the Nurse's Soul a Second Dose' (*Crisis Bridge*). She has over 10 publishing credits for her articles and poems appearing in Decision, Evangel, Women of Spirit, Upper Room and more.
Jeri is using the stepping stones of her life to soar into her destiny, while helping others along the way!

A Prayer for You

Father, I pray that your strength, comfort and peace will flow into the lives of my seasoned single brothers and sisters who may or may not be reading this book. Go before them and make all their crooked places straight. Lead to repentance unto salvation anyone that has not experienced the beauty of being adopted by You.

I pray that You, Holy Spirit will strengthen, counsel, teach and keep those who are living single and trusting in You for wisdom and guidance. Silence the negative voice of satan that torment them with lies that they are too old and need to let go of any hope of a rewarding marriage. Direct men and women onto their path that will accelerate the fulfillment of their divine purpose and destiny that they will experience the ultimate reward— hereafter eternally in Your presence.

I pray that you meet every need in this reader's life according to your riches in glory. Impart spiritual discernment along with a willing and obedient spirit that satanic pitfalls may be avoided. I plead the Blood of Jesus over all satanic assignments and any satanic covenants they may have entered knowing or unknowingly.

Father, I pray that you will quiet the voice of the enemy whispering deceitful lies into the ears of single people desiring to serve you. Let God arise and His enemies be scattered! Let them hear your voice clearly. Strengthen them with might by your Spirit in their inner man. I pray that you grant the desires of their hearts.

**In Jesus Name,
Amen**

Write YOUR Personal Prayer

OTHER TITLES BY JERI DARBY

STEPPING STONES
REFLECTIONS FOR SINGLES

VOLUME I

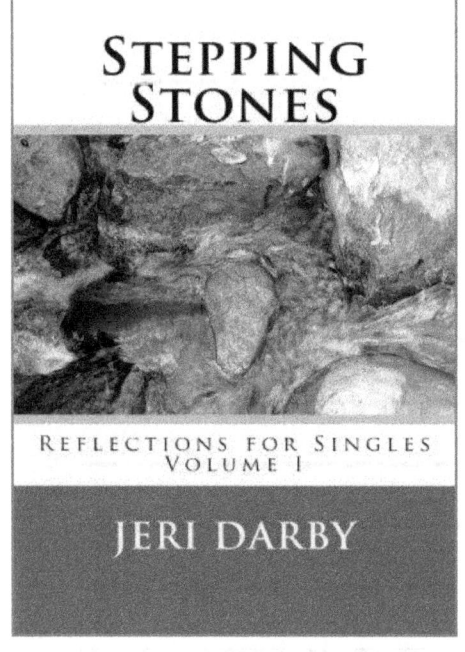

Also available in Spanish!

AVAILABLE ON AMAZON-ALSO IN KINDLE
OR VISIT ONLINE STORE
https://squareup.com/store/ararity-press/

THIS BOOK UNVEILS ERRONEOUS BELIEFS ABOUT UNFORGIVENESS AND OFFERS STRATEGIES TO APPROACH OTHERS RELATED TO THIS ISSUE.

**CONTACT JERI IF YOU WOULD LIKE TO HOST A FORGIVENESS BOOTCAMP
1 DAY, WEEKEND OR SIX WEEKS SESSIONS**

GOD LOVES ME! CELLULITE & ALL

Also available in Spanish!

GOD LOVES ME! CELLULITE IS ALL IS AN ILLUSTRATED POEM DEDICATED TO EVERY WOMAN STRUGGLING WITH WEIGHT ISSUES AND HAS QUESTIONED GOD'S LOVE.

AVAILABLE ON AMAZON-ALSO IN KINDLE OR VISIT ONLINE STORE
https://squareup.com/store/ararity-press/

**THANK YOU!
FOR PURCHASING
SEASONED FOR THIS SEASON
REFLECTIONS FOR *SEASONED* SINGLES**

**I PRAY THAT THIS BOOK HAS OFFERED COMFORT, HOPE & INSPIRATION TO STRENGTHEN YOUR JOURNEY.
WHATEVER SEASON OF LIFE YOU ARE IN, REMEMBER THAT GOD HAS NEED OF YOU!**

YOU *ARE* SEASONED FOR *THIS* SEASON!

**WATCH FOR MORE
"SEASONED FOR THIS SEASON" TITLES**

**BY
JERI DARBY**

CONTACT JERI DARBY TO SPEAK AT YOUR UPCOMING EVENT.
ARARITYPRESS@GMAIL.COM
989 717-1031

Facebook: Jeri Darby
Facebook Live: Seasoned for this Season Mondays 2 PM EST

www.ingramcontent.com/pod-product-compliance
Lightning Source LLC
LaVergne TN
LVHW061214060426
835507LV00016B/1929